942.05

D0476645

# digging deeper 2 BRITAIN 1500–1750

## ALAN BROOKS-TYREMAN  JANE SHUTER  KATE SMITH

THOMAS TAL S SCHOOL LIBRARY

Heinemann

Heinemann Educational Publishers
Halley Court, Jordan Hill, Oxford OX2 8EJ
a division of Reed Educational & Professional Publishing Ltd
Heinemann is a registered trademark of Reed Educational & Professional Publishing Ltd

OXFORD MELBOURNE AUCKLAND
JOHANNESBURG BLANTYRE GABORONE
IBADAN PORTSMOUTH NH (USA) CHICAGO

© Heinemann Educational Publishers 2000

**Copyright notice**

All rights reserved. No part of this publication may be reproduced in any material form (including photocopying or storing it in any medium by electronic means and whether or not transiently or incidentally to some other use of this publication) without the prior written permission of the copyright owner, except in accordance with the provisions of the Copyright, Designs and Patents Act 1988 or under the terms of a licence issued by the Copyright Licensing Agency Ltd, 90 Tottenham Court Road, London W1P 0LP. Applications for the copyright owner's written permission to reproduce any part of this publication should be addressed to the publisher.

First published 2000

ISBN 0 435 32770 4

02 01 00
10 9 8 7 6 5 4 3 2 1

Designed and produced by Gecko Limited, Bicester, Oxon

Original illustrations © Heinemann Educational Publishers 2000

Illustrated by Mike Spoor and Geoff Ward

Printed and bound in Spain by Mateu Cromo

Picture research by Jennifer Johnson

**Photographic acknowledgements**

The authors and publisher would like to thank the following for permission to reproduce photographs:

AKG London: 56D
Bodleian Library: 35B
Bridgeman Art Library: 7K, 19C
British Library: 40A, 41B, 50A
British Museum: 60B
Cheltenham Art Gallery and Museum/Bridgeman Art Library: 31B
Fitzwilliam Museum/Bridgeman Art Library: 26B
Giraudon, Paris: 53D
Kimbell Art Museum, Texas/Bridgeman Art Library: 42C
Mansell: 48F
Mary Evans: 38B, 39C, 54A
Methuen Collection: 7L
Mexicolore/Sean Sprague: 47C
Museo e Nazionale di Capodimonte, Naples/Bridgeman Art Library: 55B
Museum of London/Bridgeman Art Library: 62D
National Portrait Gallery: 16A, 28C, 29D
Palazzo Vecchio, Florence/Bridgeman Art Library: 24B
Pinacoteca Nazionale, Siena: 6J
Private Collection/Bridgeman Art Library: 25C, 61C
Robert Harding: 45C
Royal College of Surgeons, London: 30A
The Berger Collection, Denver Art Museum USA/Bridgeman Art Library: 12F
The Royal Collection 2000, Her Majesty the Queen: 27D
Wellcome Institute: 32C
Cover photograph: The National Gallery

The publisher has made every effort to trace the copyright holders, but if they have inadvertently overlooked any, they will be pleased to make the necessary arrangements at the first opportunity.

# CONTENTS

008765

## HISTORICAL SKILLS

Historical enquiry – What was Elizabeth I like? . . . . . . . . . . . . . . . . . . . . . . . . 4

Understanding attitudes – The poor in Elizabethan England . . . . . . . . . . . . 8

Interpretation in history – Oliver Cromwell, 'saint or sinner'? . . . . . . . . . . . .10

Understanding causes – Causes of the English Civil War . . . . . . . . . . . . . . . 14

Diaries as historical sources – Samuel Pepys and John Evelyn . . . . . . . . . . . 18

Writing a report – Massacre at Glencoe 1692 . . . . . . . . . . . . . . . . . . . . . . . 21

## DIGGING DEEPER

The man who liked experiments . . . . . . . . . . . . . . . . . . . . . . . . . . . . . . . . . 24

Harrington's toilet . . . . . . . . . . . . . . . . . . . . . . . . . . . . . . . . . . . . . . . . . . . 26

Lady Jane Grey . . . . . . . . . . . . . . . . . . . . . . . . . . . . . . . . . . . . . . . . . . . . . 28

Joseph Binns, surgeon . . . . . . . . . . . . . . . . . . . . . . . . . . . . . . . . . . . . . . . . 30

Hang the witch! . . . . . . . . . . . . . . . . . . . . . . . . . . . . . . . . . . . . . . . . . . . . 34

Matthew Hopkins, witchfinder! . . . . . . . . . . . . . . . . . . . . . . . . . . . . . . . . . 38

Cony-catchers: a real threat? . . . . . . . . . . . . . . . . . . . . . . . . . . . . . . . . . . . 40

## THEMES

Discovering a new world or destroying other cultures? . . . . . . . . . . . . . . . . . 44

1500–1600: a century of religious controversy . . . . . . . . . . . . . . . . . . . . . . 50

The poor in Elizabethan times . . . . . . . . . . . . . . . . . . . . . . . . . . . . . . . . . . 54

The struggle for power in the seventeenth century . . . . . . . . . . . . . . . . . . . . 58

Glossary . . . . . . . . . . . . . . . . . . . . . . . . . . . . . . . . . . . . . . . . . . . . . . . . . . 63

# Historical enquiry – what was Elizabeth I like?

Elizabeth I is one of the 'great' figures in English history. She worked hard on her image as a queen, but it is difficult to know exactly what she was like. How can we find out?

## From what she said ...

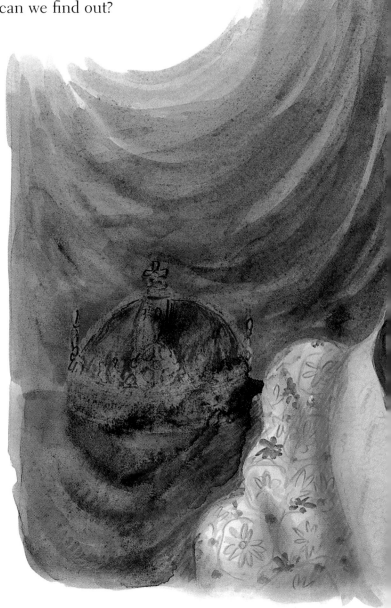

### Source A

'I know that I have the body of a weak and feeble woman, but I have the heart and stomach of a King … who should dare invade my Kingdom?'

**From Elizabeth's speech to the English Navy in 1588. It was about to take on the Spanish Armada, possibly the strongest force in Europe at that time.**

### Source B

'Must! Is "must" a word to be addressed to me? You are a little man. Your father would not have dared to use that word.'

**Elizabeth's words on her death bed to her Chief Minister, Robert Cecil. He was trying to persuade her to name a successor, since the line to the throne was not clear. Cecil's father, William, had been her adviser until 1598 and is credited with being one of England's greatest statesmen.**

### Source C

'I will make you shorter by a head!'

**This was one of Elizabeth's favourite replies when she found herself in an argument.**

### Source D

**Elizabeth had asked 18 tailors to show her designs for a new dress. Her opening words to them were:**

'Good morning, gentlemen both!'

**She was dismissing the work of most of the tailors. Elizabeth was one of the first 'power dressers' and her dresses were important to her image.**

'God may pardon (forgive) you, but I never can.'

**Elizabeth said this to the Countess of Nottingham. She was an unforgiving person. The Countess was one of her closest friends, but Elizabeth could not forgive her.**

## Work it out!

1 You are going to use all the sources to see what you can say about the personality of Elizabeth I. You are going to do **two** reports. In the first one, you are going to be critical of Elizabeth. In the second, you are going to say only good things. Include quotations in your writing.

   a The critical report might start like this:

   Elizabeth was strong-willed and refused to be told what to do. She said: 'Is "must" a word to be addressed to me?' She could also be extremely rude. Examples of this are ...

   b Now write your report just including good things.

2 You have written two completely different reports using the same information. What do you think this tells you about studying history? Here are some suggestions. Say whether you agree or disagree. Say why in each case.

   a I must have got history wrong.

   b Elizabeth must have said things which are not true.

   c History is silly because you can't get the right answer.

   d History is sometimes about interpretations and historians don't always agree.

SOURCE E

'I am your Queen. Even violence will not make me change my mind. I know what I am doing. If I was turned out of this country in my petticoat, I could live anywhere.'

**Elizabeth knew that she was popular and felt strong. She is rumoured to have said this, showing that she was a confident person.**

5

# From what people said about her ...

'She is now about 21 years old; her figure and face are very handsome. All of her actions are dignified and no one can fail to suppose she is a queen.'

**The Venetian Ambassador's description of Elizabeth.**

## Source H

'She is now 23 years old and her face is pretty rather than handsome. She is tall with a good skin. She has fine eyes and above all a beautiful hand of which she makes display. Her intelligence and understanding are wonderful. She speaks many languages, including Latin, Greek and Italian.'

**This was written by a different Venetian Ambassador two years later.**

## Source I

'Next came the Queen in her 65th year. She was very majestic (queenly). Her face was oblong. Fair but wrinkled and her eyes small yet black and pleasant. Her nose is a little hooked, her lips are narrow and her teeth are black. She wears a bright red wig.'

**A German visitor describing Elizabeth in old age. The extract is taken from a letter that he wrote.**

## Source J

Elizabeth painted in 1583.

## Work it out!

1 Look carefully at Sources G to I. Write a paragraph describing Queen Elizabeth through her life. This time, do not write a biased report. Remember to include any changes to her appearance.

# From portraits ...

Elizabeth painted in 1588.

Elizabeth painted in 1603, after her death.

## Work it out!

1 What can you learn about Elizabeth from these portraits?

2 Do you think the pictures are more useful than the written sources (A to I)? Explain your answer.

3 Can you think of any reasons why we might have to be careful about believing what we see in portraits?

4 Summary – after looking at all of the sources (A to L), what could you say if someone asked you, 'What was Elizabeth I like?'

# Understanding attitudes – the poor in Elizabethan England

During the sixteenth century the population grew, and so did the number of poor people and vagabonds. In Tudor times, a distinction was made between 'sturdy beggars' (those able to work) and the 'deserving poor' (those unable to look after themselves). Those in the first group were punished, while those in the second were given help.

Many people were frightened of gangs of wandering beggars, who they thought might bring disease to their village – or rob their homes. Elizabeth had to decide what to do about the poor. What would you have done?

SOURCE A

**A beggar being whipped through the streets.**

## SOURCE B

Some people argued that vagrants were sinners, who were out of work because God thought that they should be punished.

**From a modern school textbook.**

## SOURCE C

Vagrants shall be whipped and bored through the ear for a first offence.

Every rogue, vagabond or sturdy beggar shall be stripped naked from the middle upwards and shall be openly whipped until his back be bloody, and sent the direct way to the parish where he was born.

**Two Acts of Parliament passed in Elizabeth's reign.**

## Work it out!

You are going to write a leaflet called **What should be done about the poor?** To find out more about attitudes to the poor, read pages 42 and 55–7. You have to set out both sides of the argument – reasons for punishing the poor and reasons for helping them. Use the template below to help you. Remember that you are writing for the people of the time.

# What should be done about the poor?

## SHOULD THE POOR BE PUNISHED?

Use Sources A to C to help you think of reasons why the poor should be punished.

Add subheadings to break up your text and act as visual markers.

## SHOULD WE HELP?

Think of reasons for giving to charity or for finding jobs for the poor.

Again, add subheadings where you think they will help the reader. Use an illustration to catch people's attention.

# Interpretation in history – Oliver Cromwell, 'saint or sinner'?

On Tuesday 30 January 1649, Charles I was executed. In the months that followed, Parliament passed laws abolishing the Monarchy and set up a Commonwealth (today we would call it a republic). Both the Parliament and the army gave their support to Oliver Cromwell. Since his death in 1658, many people have debated whether Cromwell was a hero or villain. What sort of a man was he?

Some sources paint a glowing picture of Cromwell. They are very positive. Others argue that he got it wrong. They are negative. Some give a more balanced view.

In Sources A and B two historians give their views on Cromwell.

## Interpretation

In the study of history, we look at lots of sources and decide what they are telling us. For each source, we consider what may be true and what may be questioned. Then we form our own view about the person or topic. We call this 'interpretation'. Interpretation means our idea of what happened in the past, based on the evidence that we have studied.

## SOURCE A

To friendship itself he devoted much time and care and was rewarded by warmth and affection from men of many differing shades of opinion.

There was the darker side to his nature, the rage which drove him into battle, which caused him to have cut down the Irish priests without regret, have the King killed and feel not the slightest tremor afterwards. But it was a fact, generally admitted at the time, that he was not a blood-thirsty man.

**Written by the historian and novelist Antonia Fraser.**

## SOURCE B

In Irish Poetry ... he (Cromwell) sums up all that is evil in Protestantism. He is seen as somebody who is in league with the devil.

On the one hand, on a personal level, you find Cromwell in some ways an attractive figure; an informal, quite humble man.

On another level he was an absolute demon.

**The Irish historian Brendan Bradshaw in an interview.**

# Facts about Cromwell

- Cromwell was a great General. He led Parliament's army to victory in the English Civil War.

- After the execution of Charles I, in 1649, he took over the government of England.

- After the Civil War there were many rebellious groups, such as the Diggers, Levellers and Ranters. Cromwell had them crushed, even though many of them had been soldiers in his army.

- Cromwell introduced a new constitution (the rules for governing the country). It satisfied some people and angered others.

- He was one of the people who signed the death warrant of Charles I.

- Cromwell went to Ireland where there was a rebellion against the English. Cromwell had no time for rebels and treated the Irish harshly. He has been held responsible for the massacre at Drogheda in September 1649. About 2000 Irish people were murdered in a church where they had fled for safety.

- In 1657, he was offered the crown of England. It was suggested that he become King. He refused, believing that he had no right to the title. Since a long and bloody war had been fought to decide who should have responsibility and power, he believed that Parliament should control the country. He accepted the title 'Lord Protector'.

THOMAS TALLIS SCHOOL LIBRARY

# Cromwell's power!

During the English Civil War, Cromwell organised the army to fight for Parliament. His army defeated the King. But within 4 years of his victory, he had dissolved (got rid of) Parliament. Without a parliament, Cromwell could be viewed as a dictator (a person with complete control over the country).

There are different accounts of what happened.

SOURCE F

A painting of Cromwell by Robert Walker, painted in 1649.

## SOURCE C

'Take away that fool's bauble, the mace (the symbol of the House of Commons). You have sat too long here for any good. Depart, I say and let us have none of you. In the name of God go!'

**Cromwell's words to Parliament in April 1653 as written by Bulstrode Whitelock – an eyewitness. He was an MP in the House of Commons at the time.**

## SOURCE D

Then walking up and down the House like a madman, and kicking the ground with his feet, he cried out, 'You are no Parliament; I will put an end to your sitting. Call them in.'

Whereupon the sergeant attending the Parliament opened the doors and two files of musketeers (men carrying large and powerful guns) entered the House. Cromwell told the MPs to go.

**An extract from an alternative account of Cromwell dismissing Parliament in April 1653. It has been simplified for easier reading.**

## SOURCE E

Lord General Cromwell came to the House of Commons. After a while he got up. He spoke of the good things that Parliament had done, then he began pacing the floor and said, 'You are no Parliament; I will end your term in office.'

Then he said to Colonel Harrison, 'Call them in!'

**Another simplified account of Cromwell dismissing Parliament.**

# Work it out!

1  Study Sources A and B looking for the words used to describe Cromwell. Arrange the words under these two headings: **Words which show Cromwell was popular** and **Words which show Cromwell was unpopular**.

2  Use the words that you found to write a description of Cromwell. Structure your writing into three paragraphs.

   a  In the first paragraph, use the words from the 'popular' list.

   b  In the second paragraph, use the words from the 'unpopular' list.

   c  Finally, write a third paragraph giving your own views. Refer to the **Facts about Cromwell** to support your views.

3  Sources C, D and E all describe the same event but they have similarities and differences. Explore the similarities and differences by copying and completing the chart shown below.

4  Now think about why there might be similarities and differences between the sources. For each source, try to answer these questions:

   a  Do we know who wrote the source?

   b  Do we know when the source was written?

   c  Do we know if the source has been edited?

   You also need to think about these questions:

   d  Which sources use the most emotional words?

   e  Which source gives the fullest account?

5  You have looked at modern sources and historical sources which seem to tell you different things about Cromwell. You have tried to interpret all of these sources (look back at the **Interpretation** box on page 10 to make sure you know what this means). Why do you think that opinions are still split today over the question of whether Cromwell was a 'saint' or a 'sinner'?

| | Source A | Source B | Source C |
|---|---|---|---|
| Cromwell told Parliament to go | | | |
| Cromwell ordered the mace to be taken away | | | |
| He was very angry with Parliament | | | |
| He was fair and also talked about the good things that Parliament had done | | | |
| He acted like a madman | | | |
| He used soldiers to dismiss the Members of Parliament | | | |
| He argued that Parliament had done no good | | | |

# Understanding causes – Causes of the English Civil War

Events in history are very rarely caused by one single thing. Usually, an event is caused by a combination of factors. Some of these factors may build up slowly over time. These would be long-term causes. Other causes might happen suddenly, just before the event itself. These would be short-term causes. There are also other ways of dividing causes – causes can be social, political, religious, military or economic, for example.

Let's look at the long-term and short-term causes of the English Civil War.

## Long-term causes of the English Civil War

As we have seen, the English Civil War began when Oliver Cromwell led Parliament's army against the King, Charles I, and his forces.

1. King Charles I believed that God had given him the power to rule England. He thought he was more important than Parliament.
2. The power of people, such as noblemen, bishops, rich landowners and some merchants, had grown under the Tudors and it continued to be important. They wished to have more say in Parliament.
3. England was a Protestant country and Charles married a French princess who was a Catholic. Many members of Parliament and his subjects feared this was a sign he might become Catholic.
4. In 1629 Charles I decided to rule the country without the help of Parliament, which was pressing him for reforms. He would take complete control. However, legally he needed Parliament's approval to raise taxes.
5. Charles introduced a new tax called 'Ship Money'. He had the right to do this without Parliament's consent, but only in times of war and from counties by the coast. The money was supposed to be used to build new warships. England was not at war but Charles demanded payment from the whole country. He used the money instead of the taxes Parliament would have given.
6. Archbishop Laud, who had been appointed by Charles, started to change church decorations and services. This angered people who thought that Charles and Laud were trying to bring back the Catholic faith.
7. Charles was King of England and Scotland. In 1637 he introduced a new prayer book in Scotland, one that was less strictly Protestant than the old one. This angered the Scots, and they rioted. Charles decided to send an army to Scotland to stop the rebellion.

8. To pay for this army, Charles tried to raise another tax called 'Coat and Conduct Money'. Legally, he was allowed to do this only if the country was at war with another country. Many people refused to pay.

9. In November 1640, Charles was so desperate for money that he had to call Parliament together. Charles could not collect most kinds of taxes without the permission of Parliament.

10. Legally, Charles had to do what Parliament wanted.

11. Parliament demanded that it should be allowed to meet regularly. It had not met for 11 years.

12. A second demand was that Archbishop Laud's unpopular changes to religion should be abolished (got rid of).

13. Charles and Parliament reached a compromise (they met each other half way) in 1641. Charles agreed that Parliament would be allowed to meet every 3 years. Parliament gave permission for Charles to raise some taxes.

# Work it out!

1 The causes listed can be divided into three types:

   a **Economic causes**

   b **Political causes**

   c **Religious causes**.

Organise the causes into the three categories.

2 Now you have sorted the causes into three different types, you are ready to produce a piece of extended writing. Try to answer the question below using the writing frame to help you.

'The long-term causes of the English Civil War were mainly religious.' Do you agree with this statement?

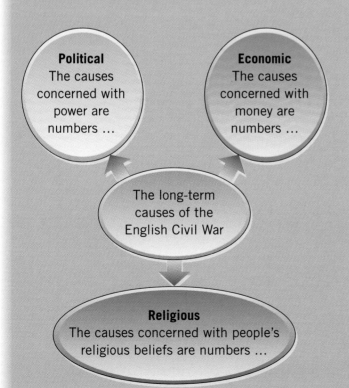

**Political**
The causes concerned with power are numbers …

**Economic**
The causes concerned with money are numbers …

The long-term causes of the English Civil War

**Religious**
The causes concerned with people's religious beliefs are numbers …

The religious causes of the Civil War were …

The political causes of the Civil War were more or less important because …

The economic causes were more or less important because …

I do/do not think that religion was the most important long-term cause of the Civil War.

# Short-term causes of the English Civil War

By the summer of 1641 it looked as though the King and Parliament would be able to work together. A year later, on 22 August 1642, war broke out. How had the country gone from peace to war?

The events from late 1641 to August 1642 are the short-term causes of the Civil War.

The Grand Remonstrance listed the problems that Charles I and the bishops had caused Parliament in the past. It also set out Parliament's request for more control over religious and political discussions in the future. It showed that Parliament did not trust the King to continue to share power.

Charles I, painted by Daniel Mytens in 1631.

1.  In November 1641, Parliament made a set of demands. Many MPs wanted a reduction in the power of the bishops. The bishops acted as advisers to Charles I and Parliament didn't like this. The demands are known as the Grand Remonstrance. The vote to pass the Grand Remonstrance was very close and it split Parliament.
2.  In the same month, there was a rebellion in Ireland. Catholics killed Protestants. People began to worry about religious divisions.
3.  In January 1642, Charles burst into Parliament with 400 soldiers. He demanded the arrest of five leading MPs who he saw as trouble-makers. The MPs escaped. People felt that Charles had gone too far.
4.  An army had to be sent to Ireland to put down the uprising. The King had always controlled the army. However, the MPs did not trust Charles and believed that he might use the army against them. So, Parliament took control of the army.

5. On 1 June 1642, Parliament issued a new set of demands. This split MPs into two groups – those who supported the King and those who did not.
6. Parliament ordered each county to raise an army.
7. Charles I made the same demand and so people had to make a choice – to fight for the King or to fight for Parliament.
8. Charles lost control of London and fled. On 22 August 1642, he raised his standard at Nottingham, a safe royalist town. He declared war on Parliament's army and the Civil War began.

## Work it out!

1 A Venn diagram is a way of presenting information which you have sorted into separate groups. It allows you to show, visually, which information is in which group – and if any information can be placed in more than one group. Use the template for a Venn diagram to organise the short-term causes into three, possibly overlapping, categories: religious, political and military (about the army) causes.

2 So, what were the short-term causes of the English Civil War? Write a paragraph on each of the three types of causes that you have identified.

3 Try to say whether the long-term or the short-term causes were more important.

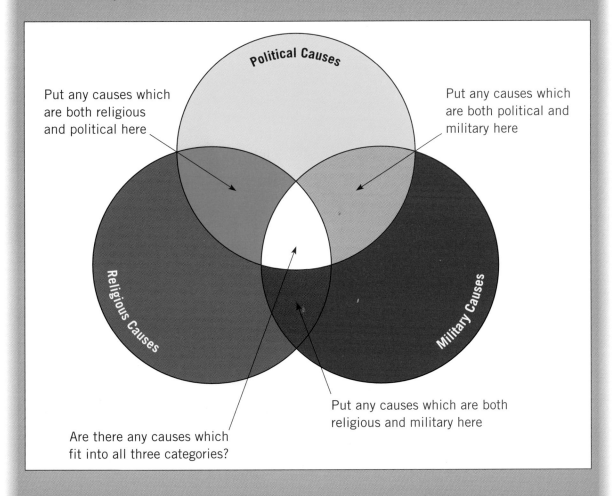

Political Causes

Put any causes which are both religious and political here

Put any causes which are both political and military here

Religious Causes

Military Causes

Put any causes which are both religious and military here

Are there any causes which fit into all three categories?

# Diaries as historical sources – Samuel Pepys and John Evelyn

Diaries can be useful sources but we need to be very careful how we analyse them. Some diaries are very personal and some are written as public records. All diaries reflect the writer's own point of view. So, we need to think about the person who kept the diary and why he or she wrote it, as well as the events described in it, keeping in mind what we already know about the historical period.

## The plague and Samuel Pepys

Much of our knowledge about the plague comes from the diaries of Samuel Pepys. Pepys began writing his diary in 1660 and he had plenty of interesting things to comment on. The first entry was made on 1 January 1660. Perhaps it was Pepys' New Year resolution to write a diary!

Within a few years Pepys had witnessed the Great Plague and the Great Fire of London. He continued to write his diaries throughout his career and into his later life. He stopped keeping a diary in May 1669 because his eyesight had become too poor to write.

When he died in 1703, his diaries were left to Magdalene College, Cambridge. The only problem was that he had written in a special form of shorthand which no one could read! Pepys wanted his diaries to be completely private. He certainly did not want his wife to read them. He had been unfaithful to her and had named other people who had been involved in scandals. It was not until 1822 that the diaries were decoded and a colourful picture of life in mid-seventeenth-century London emerged.

| | |
|---|---|
| *15 June 1665* | London grows very sickly, and people are afraid of it. |
| *17 June 1665* | Going in a Hackney coach from Holborn, the coachman I found to drive very badly. At last he stopped, and came down hardly able to stand. He told me that he was suddenly taken very ill and almost blind, and that he could not see. So I got down and went to another coach, with a sad heart for the poor man and fear for myself, in case he had been struck with the plague … But God have mercy upon us all. |
| *21 June 1665* | I find all the town almost going out of town, the coaches and wagons being full of people going into the country. |
| *22 June 1665* | In great pain whether to send my mother into the country today or no … I resolved to put it to her, and she agreed to go. |
| *29 June 1665* | By water to Whitehall, where the court (of Charles II) is ready to go out of town. This end of town everyday grows very bad of the plague. |
| *30 June 1665* | Considered removing my wife (Elizabeth) to Woolwich … |

**Extracts from Samuel Pepys' diary for 1665.**

A man of abounding (huge amounts of) love of life who gave us a vivid (very clear) picture of his life.

**Pepys, as described in *Chambers Biographical Dictionary*.**

Samuel Pepys.

# John Evelyn

John Evelyn lived in Deptford in London. He also kept a diary, between 1641 and 1706. His writing contains many colourful descriptions of famous people who lived at that time. He spent a lot of time at the court of Charles II and also knew the Tsar (King) of Russia, Peter the Great. Evelyn rented out his house to Peter the Great. He disliked the Russian Tsar because he made such a mess of his home.

Evelyn's diaries were found by chance in 1817, over 100 years after his death. They were in an old clothes basket at his home in Wooton!

SOURCE D

| | |
|---|---|
| *2 August 1665* | A solemn fast through England to plead against God's displeasure against the people. |
| *28 August 1665* | The disease still increasing. I sent my wife and whole family to my brother's at Wooton. |
| *7 September 1665* | The streets now thin of people; the shops shut up. |
| *11 October 1665* | Multitudes of poor creatures begging for alms … |
| *6 February 1666* | My wife and family returned … from the country. |

**Extracts from John Evelyn's diary, 1665–1666.**

# Work it out!

1 When analysing diaries it is helpful to think about four different aspects: who the author was, who the intended audience was, the context (what it was like at the time of writing) and the content of the writing (what the diary is about). Use the following questions and the other sources to help you analyse Source A.

  a Author
   • Do we know anything about the author of the diary?
   • Why did the author write the diary?

  b Audience
   • Who did the author intend to read his diary?
   • Was it supposed to be kept secret?

  c Context
   • Was the writer living in London at the time?
   • Did he write the evidence at the time?

  d Content
   • What does the source tell us about the events of 1665?

2 Use the same headings and questions to evaluate (weigh up the strengths and weaknesses) of John Evelyn's diary, Source D.

3 Are there points of agreement between the two diary extracts (Sources A and D)?

4 Are diaries a useful form of historical evidence?

# Writing a report – Massacre at Glencoe 1692

Glencoe is a remote mountain pass in the Highlands of Scotland. In 1692 it was the scene of a great massacre. On the King's instructions, members of the Campbell clan were stationed in the houses of their enemies, the MacDonalds of Glencoe. Then, in the early hours of the morning of 13 February, the Campbells turned on the families with whom they were staying, killing men, women and children.

Why did this happen? The sources below will help you understand more fully.

## SOURCE A

### The new King

King James II was forced to give up the throne by William III in 1688. James had supporters in Scotland. William wanted to make sure that all the chiefs in Scotland were loyal to him and not to James. He promised to forget any past rebellions if they swore an oath of loyalty by 1 January 1692.

### The MacDonalds in trouble

Alexander MacDonald of Glencoe did take the oath but bad weather meant that he was a few days late. The government wrote a letter which allowed the MacDonalds to be attacked, using force.

### Murder by the Campbells

A hundred soldiers of Clan Campbell, enemies of the MacDonalds, were sent to live in Glencoe with MacDonald families for over a week. Suddenly, the Campbells attacked the MacDonalds in their beds, and the Clan chief, 30 of his men, two women and two children were killed.

### The truth?

It is now thought that the leader of Clan Campbell and the government minister for Scotland were behind the plot. King William did not order the killings, but he was guilty because he never punished anyone for the massacre.

**The story of the Glencoe Massacre from a recent school textbook.**

## SOURCE B

You are hereby ordered and authorised to act against these Highland rebels who have not taken the benefit of our indemnity, by fire and sword and all manner of hostility; to burn their houses, seize or destroy their goods or cattle, plenishings or clothes, and to cut off the men.

**Part of a letter sent by William III to the Secretary for Scotland on 11 January 1692. The King's orders also said that mercy should be shown to those who had not taken the oath, as long as they now did so.**

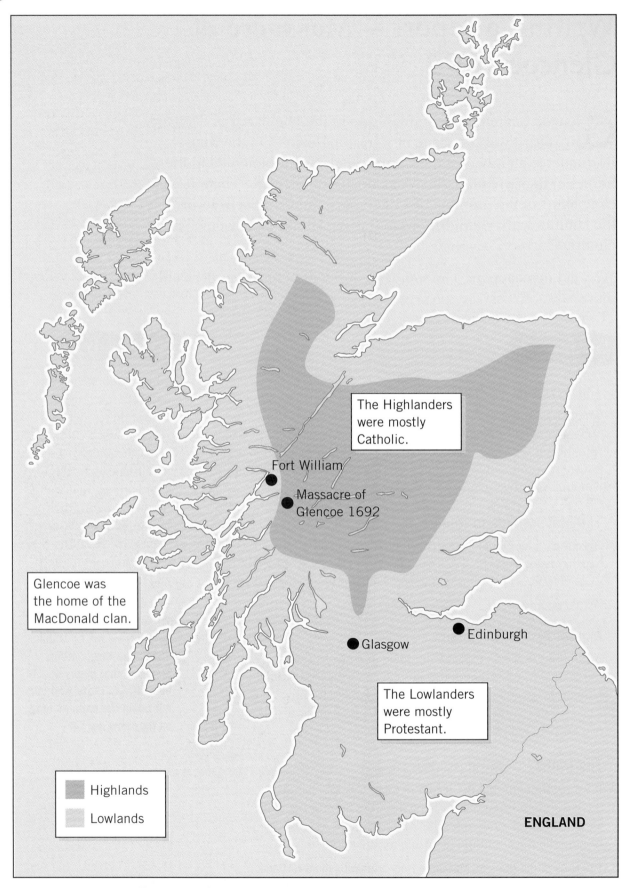

The Highlanders were mostly Catholic.

Glencoe was the home of the MacDonald clan.

Fort William

Massacre of Glencoe 1692

The Lowlanders were mostly Protestant.

● Edinburgh

● Glasgow

Highlands
Lowlands

ENGLAND

A map of Scotland showing the loyalties of the Highland and Lowland Scots, taken from a book called *Folklore, Myths and Legends*, published in 1977.

## SOURCE C

On 29 December, MacDonald, the chief of the MacDonald family, rode through a snow storm from Glencoe to Fort William to take his oath of loyalty to the King. But the Governor told him that the oath had to be taken before the Sheriff at Inverary – 60 miles away. So MacDonald rode on and reached Inverary on 2 January. But the Sheriff was away celebrating New Year and MacDonald was not able to make his oath until 6 January.

The delay allowed William III the chance to give the Highlanders a lesson for their previous support for James II. William ordered that 120 soldiers, mostly from the Campbell clan, should be stationed in the MacDonalds' houses in Glencoe. The Campbells were enemies of the MacDonalds, but they were accepted because Highland custom said that fighting had to stop. For two weeks the Campbells lived with the MacDonalds until the message came that all MacDonalds under 70 should be put to the sword. At 5 a.m. on 13 February, the killing of men, women and children began. Some escaped the massacre, only to freeze to death in the Highland snow. The attack was a failure. Only 38 bodies were found – less than a tenth of the MacDonald clan. But the Highland Scots had seen how cruel the English could be and this merely added to the support which the exiled James II and his descendants received in later years.

**From a modern school textbook.**

## SOURCE D

The MacDonalds were killed by the Campbell clan. The Campbells were acting on the orders of William III. To this day, legends about the Glencoe Massacre live on. One story tells how a Campbell soldier was sickened by an order to murder a woman and her child in the snow. He killed a wolf instead, and showed his blood-stained sword to his officer, to make him think he had obeyed.

**From a modern source.**

# Work it out!

Now you are going to use all the sources to write your own report on the massacre at Glencoe. Use the instructions below to help you.

1  Write a headline for your report. Make sure that it will grab the reader's attention.

2  Write a paragraph on the long-term causes of the massacre. The section headed 'The new King' in Source A will be useful. You could also refer to the map on page 22.

3  Try to explain the short-term causes of the massacre. Include the government's letter and the role of the Campbell clan. Again, Source A will help you.

4  Write a paragraph on MacDonald's attempt to swear loyalty to William III. Look at Sources B and C.

5  Using all the sources, explain what actually happened at Glencoe. Say who was behind the plot. Use 'The truth?', Source A.

6  Use Source C to help you explain the consequences of the massacre.

# The man who liked experiments

Sir Francis Bacon was one of the first seventeenth-century scientists to say that the study of science should not just reuse the work of previous scientists. Bacon insisted that scientists should experiment, observe and record things for themselves.

## Bacon's view of science

Scientists should work out what they want to study. Then they should:

- plan the best experiments to help them understand what they are studying
- set up the experiments
- observe the results
- record the results.

This sounds obvious now, as it is the way we are taught science, but it was revolutionary at the time. In Bacon's time, people simply memorised existing books.

SOURCE B

**Seventeenth-century scientists had not yet drawn a dividing line between magic and science. They believed anything was possible. Many of them spent a great deal of time and money trying to turn iron into gold, for instance, as shown in this painting from the time, called 'Alchemy'.**

SOURCE A

Bacon's aim was to create a 'new learning'. He believed that reforming scientific methods would improve all kinds of learning. Yet, he was not a professional scientist. His knowledge of science was patchy and his experimental ideas were over-simple.

Bacon was a lawyer, busily trying to be successful at the royal court. It was not until he was disgraced (for taking bribes as a judge) that he concentrated on, and wrote seriously about, science.

**Written by the historian Marie Boas in 1962.**

# An experimental death

This story of Bacon's death, at the age of 65, comes from the seventeenth-century 'biographer' John Aubrey. Aubrey was more interested in gossip and a good story than accurate information. However, Thomas Hobbes, a good friend of Bacon, told Aubrey the story. Most historians accept it as true.

Bacon was driving in a coach with a Dr Winterbourne towards Highgate, London. It was a wintry day and he began to think about snow. Was it possible that snow could preserve meat, in the way that salt did? He discussed the idea with Winterbourne. They decided to experiment at once. They made the coachman stop the coach at the bottom of Highgate Hill, beside some cottages. They went to the first cottage. The woman who lived there was poor, so was glad to sell them one of her hens. They gave her far more than it was worth for killing, plucking and gutting it straight away. Then they went outside and stuffed the chicken with snow. It was not until the chicken was stuffed that Bacon realised he was very cold and wet. Rather than travel all the way back to his home in London in an unheated coach, he decided to go to the home of his friend Lord Arundel, which was much closer. He kept a tight hold on the chicken all the way. Lord Arundel was not there but the servants knew Bacon and let him in, putting him to bed on the doctor's orders. Although the servants had warmed the bed carefully before Bacon got into it, no one had slept in the room for so long that the bed was damp. He caught bronchitis and died several days later. The letter he dictated to his friend, explaining why he had come to the house, ended with: 'As for the experiment itself, it succeeded excellently well.' These are his last known words.

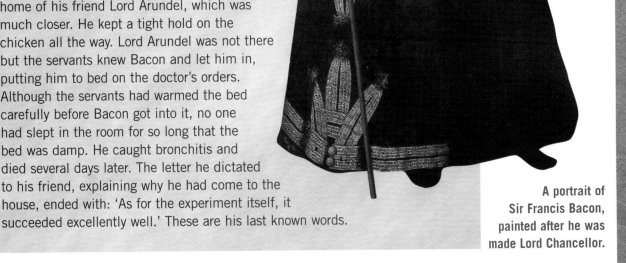

**A portrait of Sir Francis Bacon, painted after he was made Lord Chancellor.**

## Work it out!

'Bacon wasn't a proper scientist, he's not important. He was just playing at science, the way a kid plays. Look at the chicken story, and the fact he only wrote about science once he lost all his jobs.'

'Bacon's ideas about experiments made him one of the first people to think about science in the way that we still do today. That makes him very important.'

Which statement do you agree with? Explain why.

# Harrington's toilet

In 1596, Sir John Harrington, godson of Queen Elizabeth I, made a plumbing breakthrough. He invented the flushing toilet. The very first working example was built for him at his home in Kelston, near Bath. The only other one was installed in Richmond Palace, for his godmother's use. But the invention never caught on. Why not?

It was not as if there was no need for better sewage disposal! One of the reasons the Tudor Court moved from palace to palace, was to give the servants a chance to clean and air the rooms. While the royal palaces did have 'privies' (toilets), male courtiers often urinated in quiet corners rather than walk to the privy. Privies were located, for obvious reasons, some distance from the rooms used daily by the Queen and her Court. Buckets and chamber pots were also used, but could be spilt or kicked over. The rushes on the floor became soaked with old food, grease and other spillages.

Some privies were built over a cesspit, which would eventually fill and need cleaning. In the case of Hampton Court it was the moat, over which the privies were built, that needed clearing.

## SOURCE A

'You should make your invention generally known. It would give pleasure to a great many persons. It would also do Her Majesty a great service in her palace of Greenwich and other stately houses, that are often annoyed with smells which, where mouths are fed, cannot be avoided.'

**Advice given to Sir John Harrington in a pamphlet by 'a friend' writing under the name of Philostilpnos.**

Nonsuch Palace was one of Queen Elizabeth's favourite homes. Courtiers liked it less. It was so small that many people had to camp outside, in tents, and the sanitary arrangements were even worse than usual.

## SOURCE B

To work adequately, a toilet needs not only a flushing mechanism but a ready supply of water for flushing and a sewer to take the flushings away. Harrington did not concern himself with these things – he left that to the builder of the closet. Most homes did not have piped water. Water had to be carried in buckets from the nearest stream or well. It was trouble enough providing the water for cooking and washing, without bringing more for luxuries like water closets.

**Written by the historian Terence McLaughlin in 1971.**

## Harrington's instructions

- Make an oval bowl of brick, stone or lead, as wide at the bottom as at the top, measuring 60 cm deep, 30 cm wide and 40 cm long. It must slope to the right. Line it with pitch, resin and wax, to make it waterproof.

- Make an 8 cm inlet at the back, set just below the top, with a brass outlet joined to a small lead pipe which runs up to a cistern in the room above, or as high as is convenient, which is to have a constant supply of water. Water is let down from the cistern to the pipe and bowl by using a washer to open or shut the pipe.

- In the lowest part of the bowl, on the right, make an exit hole some 6 cm across. This must lead to a pipe to carry the water away, which drops steeply as soon as it may.

- The pipe from the bowl must have a strong sluice to hold the water back or let it through, which is controlled by a screw-type key.

- When the dirty water has been let out, at least a foot of clean water should be run into the bowl, to stop smells.

**A close stool used by both Elizabeth I and James I in Hampton Court. This was a chair with a lidded section containing a removable pot or bucket that was emptied regularly by servants.**

## Sewage disposal

Nowhere, not even the royal palaces or the bustling town of London, had a system of drains for sewage. Sewage was tipped into streets and rivers. Cesspits were emptied infrequently. Some places that used urine as a bleach, such as laundries, collected and paid for saved urine. But, especially in growing towns, it was hard to cope with the amount of sewage.

## Work it out!

1  Draw a labelled diagram of Harrington's water closet.

2  Why did it not become a huge success?

Explain your answer, referring to the sources and information in this unit.

# Lady Jane Grey

Lady Jane Grey, a Protestant, had the misfortune to live at a time of religious upheaval. Edward VI, the dying King, was her cousin and also a Protestant. His sister, Mary, next in line to rule, was a Catholic. The Duke of Northumberland, Edward's powerful adviser, did not want a Catholic to rule. He persuaded Edward to make Jane his heir. Jane's parents forced her to marry Guildford Dudley, the Duke of Northumberland's son.

Edward died on 6 July 1553. On 10 July Lady Jane Grey was proclaimed Queen, despite making it clear that she did not want to rule. Preparations began for her coronation. She was only 16 years old. The Duke of Northumberland hoped people would accept Jane as Queen, because of her religion. He was wrong. Mary raised an army and marched on London, gathering support, even from non-Catholics, as she came.

It was all over by 3 August. Jane's father, who had pressed her so hard to take the throne, now told her to give it up to Mary. The Duke of Northumberland announced that he supported Mary after all. He even became a Catholic, in the hope of saving his life. He failed and was executed on 22 August. Jane was arrested and imprisoned in the Tower of London. Many who had urged Jane to take the throne now did all they could to gain Mary's favour, even changing their religion. Jane and her husband, Guildford, were executed on 11 February 1554. Her father was executed 2 weeks later.

## SOURCE A

*Sir,*

*I find this request easier to fulfil than my advancement to royalty. Out of obedience to you and my mother, I have sinned and done myself harm. I willingly, following the bidding of my own soul, give up the crown.*

**Taken from a letter from Jane to her father, in reply to his letter urging her to give up the throne.**

## SOURCE B

*Father,*

*Although it has pleased God to hasten my death, yet I rejoice in my mishaps, knowing that I am innocent and that my guiltless blood may cry before the Lord, 'Mercy to the innocent'.*

**Taken from a letter from Jane to her father, written shortly before her execution.**

## SOURCE C

**A sixteenth-century portrait of Lady Jane Grey.**

An early Victorian painting of the execution of Lady Jane Grey.

# Images of Jane

In death, as in life, Lady Jane Grey was manipulated. People used parts of her story to represent her in the way they wanted. There were three main images of her:

- **The innocent** – popular songs written after her death showed Jane and Guildford Dudley as two innocents, forced by the Duke of Northumberland into actions that would lead to their deaths. (This view completely ignores the fact that Dudley joined with everyone else in pressing Jane to be Queen – he wanted to rule.)

- **The Protestant martyr** – Mary Tudor certainly promised that Jane would be spared execution if she changed her faith. Whether Mary would have kept her word and allowed Jane to live, as a possible focus for rebellion, is less clear.

- **The clever, dutiful girl** – this image of Jane is as a bookish and thoughtful girl. Rather than going to her doom unawares, or through a desire to stay Protestant, she goes knowing what will probably happen, but doing her duty to her parents.

## Work it out!

1 Which image(s) of Jane do her letters support? Why do you think this?

2 Which image(s) of Jane does Source D support? Why do you think this?

3 Sources C and D give very different images of Jane.
   a Why do you think this is?
   b Which do you think is most likely to be right?

Explain your answers.

29

# Joseph Binns, surgeon

What was it like to be a seventeenth-century surgeon? Did you have to have special training? What injuries did you treat and how did you treat them?

Joseph Binns was a surgeon in London from the 1630s until his death in 1664. His medical notes for the years 1633 to 1663 have survived. He records details of the patient, the problem, what he did and what the results of his treatment were. Some of the notes are very brief: 'A girl in Shoe Lane put her right elbow out. Put it in. Well.' Others go into more detail, as we shall see. But first we need to find out how Binns became a surgeon.

Surgeons needed a licence to work. They could get this by studying at university, or by joining a surgeons' guild and working as an apprentice to a licensed surgeon. Binns became an apprentice to the London surgeon Joseph Fenton in 1633. The London guild, the Company of Barbers and Surgeons, was one of the best run guilds. There were lectures for its members. It had strict rules and punished its members for breaking them.

This painting shows Henry VIII giving the Company of Barbers and Surgeons their Charter in 1540. (A charter is a special document which describes the rules of an organisation.) The Company's hospitals in London, St Bartholomew's and St Thomas's, were the first English hospitals to see their job as looking after the sick, not just giving shelter and all kinds of care to the poor.

## A family man?

Binns' notes tell us very little about his personal life. From his will and his notes we know that he was born in Derbyshire and moved to London when he became an apprentice to Joseph Fenton in 1633.

By 1648, he was one of three surgeons at St Bartholomew's Hospital, earning £30 a year (a skilled craftsman would have been earning about £10 a year, a labourer just over £2). By this time, he had also married Mary Holland and was running his own practice, living in a house in Butchers Hall Lane, London. He and Mary had at least two sons and a daughter. He left sets of surgical instruments to his sons in his will, hoping they would become surgeons like him. The elder, Fenton, did. By the time Binns died, he had earned enough money to buy property in Oxfordshire, Berkshire and Middlesex. He had also lent money which was being repaid with interest. He lent £1300 in all, a lot of money at the time.

SOURCE A

Surgeons mostly made home visits, although some patients came to the surgeon's home for the first consultation. Binns often visited his patients twice a day while he was treating them.

## Patients

Binns' patients were mostly Londoners, although some came to London from the country to consult him. His patients came from all social groups, ranging from Archbishops to servants, although most of his private patients were middle-class. He also treated members of his own family.

## What problems did Binns treat?

Many of the problems Binns treated were wounds of various kinds, or boils and growths that needed cutting out.

These are the ailments that surgeons were supposed to treat, according to the Charter:

- dog bites
- human bites
- gunshot wounds
- fractures
- tumours
- hernias.

- snake bites
- stab wounds
- wounds (general)
- dislocations
- ulcers

Binns also treated patients with ailments that, under the rules of the Company of Barbers and Surgeons, he was supposed to leave to a physician. These illnesses needed 'internal' not 'external' cures – that is medicine, not cutting, stitching and bandaging. Many of the patients he treated 'illegally' were family members who it would have been hard to turn away.

Illnesses that Binns treated although he was not supposed to included:

- headaches
- stomach ache
- epilepsy.

- back pain
- diarrhoea

Here are some of Binns' methods for treating his patients. All treatments were given without any anaesthetic, for none had been discovered. A glass of brandy might be given to help dull the pain, otherwise the best a patient could hope for would be to pass out quickly.

## Wounds

With a wound, Binns' first act was to stop the bleeding. He stitched up small wounds as soon as the bleeding stopped. He put ointment on them, to try to stop infection. With larger wounds, he searched inside for any objects (such as a bullet, the point of a blade or fabric from the patient's clothing). Binns knew that larger wounds often became infected, so he kept them open with a wedge of bandage. This meant that the pus from the infection could drain away. He also put ointment on, to reduce the infection. Binns made a whole range of ointments and used various ways of applying them. He seems to have been very successful in preventing infection – there are only three cases of amputation in his notes – most surgeons at the time had a far higher amputation rate. When the wounds were clear of infection or swelling, he stitched them up.

## Tumours and boils

Small boils and sores were cured simply by applying ointment. If this failed, Binns used mercury or 'caustic stone' to burn the sores away. This was painful, but then, so was any other treatment. Larger boils were cut off and tumours cut out. After this, they were treated like wounds.

## Fractures and breaks

Binns used splints, plasters and bandaging to set broken or fractured bones. First, he tried to reduce the swelling. Then he set the bones. He was concerned about getting the limb working, not making a perfect join.

## Purging, the universal cure?

Whatever he was treating, Binns also gave prescriptions to put the patient's body in the best state for recovery. He almost always purged his patients to clear their bowels, no matter what the problem. He seldom 'bled' patients, although it was his standard headache cure. Binns believed diet was important to recovery. He told patients what to eat and drink while he was treating them.

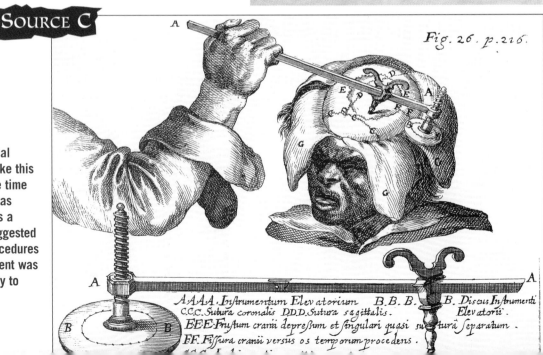

Fig. 26. p.216.

Some surgical textbooks, like this one from the time that Binns was practising as a surgeon, suggested surgical procedures that the patient was most unlikely to survive!

AAAA. Instrumentum Elevatorium    B.B.B.    B. Discus Instrumenti
C.C.C. Sutura coronalis  DDD.Sutura sagittalis.    Elevatorii.
EEE. Frustum cranii depressum et singulari quasi sutura separatum.
FF. Fissura cranii versus os temporum procedens.

Illustrations from books of surgery at the time showed the best way to repair all kinds of wounds.

## War wounds

Binns treated three soldiers who were wounded at the Battle of Newbury, 20 September 1643. One of them was his cousin, Edward Green, who brought the others with him. Green had a broken arm, which Binns set. Captain Manwaring had been shot, but his armour had stopped the bullet and he just had bad bruising, which Binns treated with ointment. Captain Broomfield had been shot twice, once through the shoulder and once through the collarbone. Binns treated the Captain successfully, although the wounds gave off 'dirty, black matter' for several days.

## Dangerous trades

Binns treated more builders than any other craftsmen, mainly for falls and for wounds from tools. A bricklayer called Myllis was particularly unlucky:

'Myllis had a severe fall from some three storeys inside a new building, through the timber floors. He was speechless for about an hour, then spoke, but not sensibly. His collarbone was broken, which I set, and he had a bump to the back of his head. He returned to work on the same building and was later found dead, perhaps from another fall.'

## Tempers fly

Many wounds that Binns treated happened as a result of drunken arguments. People carried daggers and swords at the time and a quarrel could result in stab wounds. Sometimes people resorted to their fists. They also used their teeth. Bite injuries were quite common and Binns treated three of these. In the case of a quarrel between two musicians, the bite was severe:

'Mr Ashberry was bitten by Mr Gottier, the Frenchman. The wound was an inch or more wide and ran from the corner of his mouth and bottom lip down across his cheek to the lower jaw.'

## Mrs Wilson's baby

Some cases were hopeless. When the Wilson baby was born, in January 1648, it had a small, soft tumour on the base of the skull where it joined the neck:

'This grew bigger and bigger so that in September 1648 it was as big as a fist. I diagnosed water and saw that the head itself was swelling and the skull was split. I was fearful to open the tumour, but did so at the urgings of the mother on 15 September.'

Between 15 September and 16 October Binns repeatedly reopened the tumour and drained more fluid. The baby was sick and feverish most of the time, and died on 16 October.

## Work it out!

1   **a** How did Joseph Binns treat wounds?
    **b** What was the biggest danger with wounds?

2   What do the wounds that Binns treated tell you about life in seventeenth-century England?

3   The artwork above is copied exactly from a medical book from Binns' time. How helpful do you think it would have been to someone learning surgery at that time? Explain your answer.

# Hang the witch!

## SOURCE A

A
CONFIRMATION
And Discovery of
# WITCH CRAFT,

*Containing thefe feverall particulars;*

That there are Witches called
bad Witches, and Witches untruely called
good or white Witches, and what manner of
people they be, and how they may bee knowne,
with many particulars thereunto tending.

Together with the Confeffions of many of thofe executed fince
May 1645. in the feverall Counties hereafter mentioned.
As alfo fome objections Anfwered.

By *John Stearne*, now of *Lawfhall* neere *Burie
Saint Edmonds* in *Suffolke*, fometimes of
*Manningtree* in *Effex.*

PROV.17.15. He that juftifieth the wicked, and he that condemneth the juft, even they
both are an abomination to the Lord.
DEVT. 13.14. Thou fhalt therefore inquire, and make fearch, and afke diligently,
whether it be truth, and the thing certaine.

LONDON,
Printed by *William Wilfon*, dwelling in Little Saint Bartholo-
mewes neere Smithfield. 1 6 4 8. —

**By the 1640s there were many pamphlets about witches and how to catch them.**

Sixteenth- and seventeenth-century England had several waves of witchcraft trials. There were similar trials all over Europe. When they happened, how often they occurred and whether the 'witches' were found guilty varied, depending on where and when the accusations were made. In England, there were more accusations and convictions during the 1580s and 1590s and the 1640s and 1650s than at other times. The type of person accused of witchcraft and the reasons given for the accusations were always very similar. So, who was accused of witchcraft? Why were they accused and who did the accusing?

At the time, most people believed in magic. They also believed that witches existed. People disagreed about how powerful witches were, about how they organised themselves and about how you could recognise one – but not about their existence.

## Dangerous pets

Witches were believed, more and more as the period progressed, to have made an agreement with the Devil, who gave them their powers. The Devil often came disguised as an animal, or gave each witch a spirit, or 'familiar', to do his work. These familiars were also disguised as animals. Possession of a pet was another 'proof' of being a witch.

## Who was accused?

In England, nine out of every ten of those accused of witchcraft were women. Most of them were old, widowed and poor. Many of the accused were women who did not fit in with the people of their village. Sometimes they had a physical deformity that marked them out – a squint, a squeaking voice, a limp. Beggars were less likely to be accused of witchcraft than people actually living in the community. Accusations against rich and important people were rare, as were accusations against men.

The most famous trials often involved the accusation of one woman and spread to include many of her female friends and relatives. This was especially true in the 1640s and 1650s, when witch-hunters were employed to track down witches. By this time, there were many books published on witches and how to 'detect' them. So the witch-hunters had a system of 'proofs' to work with. As witch-hunters were paid £1 or more for each witch discovered, it is not surprising that they found so many.

## 'White' witches

Magic was an accepted part of life. It was not always seen as a bad thing. 'White' witches and 'cunning men' were people who practised magic to help others. The witchcraft laws specified that those accused must be shown to have practised magic to cause harm.

**This painting shows a man joining a witches' coven.**

SOURCE B

## Accusers

People made allegations of witchcraft for a variety of reasons. But, in almost every trial, the testimony of the accuser was that he or she had recently suffered some misfortune and had had a disagreement with the accused. So what might drive people to make these accusations?

- **Spite** – people with grudges made accusations. However, the person they were accusing had to fit the commonly held view of the kind of person who was a witch. Accusations of witchcraft against rich people were unlikely to get support.

- **Self-defence** – some accusers used accusations of witchcraft to cover up something they had done wrong, or to explain why they had acted badly. A servant who did not churn the butter properly might then say it had been bewitched. Children might fail to do a given task, and use the same excuse. People from all levels of society used witchcraft as an explanation for things. As early as the 1540s, Henry VIII, tired of Anne Boleyn, used witchcraft to explain why he had married her in the first place.

- **To explain misfortune** – when bad things happen, people like to know the reason. In cases where there was no obvious explanation, people turned to supernatural causes. One way of explaining misfortunes was to say it was God's will or God's punishment. This was the reasoning that was often used to explain big, natural disasters or plagues. Witches were seldom blamed for these.

For individuals, it was far more comforting to think that a witch had singled you out for disaster, than to think that God had done so; especially if, as in the case of the Vicar of Brenchley in the 1580s, you were supposed to be God's representative on Earth. The Vicar's son had fallen sick, suddenly and unexpectedly. Rather than blaming God, the Vicar blamed Margaret Simons, 'a known witch', whose dog the boy had been chasing with a knife. The Vicar was so sure that the boy had been bewitched that he looked for a 'cunning man' who could work 'white magic' to cure him.

# Some 'witches' and their accusers

## Guilty consciences?

At this time, villagers were expected to help each other out, lending goods and giving the poor food and drink. They did not always do so. In 1579, Margery Stanton of Wimbush, near Chelmsford, was accused of witchcraft. Her accusers were:

- **Thomas Pratt**, who had snatched a handful of grain from her and fed it to his chickens. Most of these died soon after.

- **Richard Saunders' wife**, who had refused to lend Margery any yeast and whose child suddenly and 'in a marvellous strange manner' fell sick.

- **Robert Petie's wife**, who had refused to give Margery a drink of water and whose child suddenly fell sick.

- **The Vicar's wife**, who had refused to give Margery food or drink and whose child suddenly fell sick.

- **Robert Cornell and his wife**, who had refused to give Margery a drink of milk. Robert's cows' milk turned to blood and his wife grew a tumour.

- **John Hopwood**, who refused to lend her a leather thong and whose horse died soon after, very suddenly.

- **Robert Lathbury**, who 'refused her request'. Twenty of his pigs died soon after, very suddenly.

## Witch-hunters

Although witch-hunters were paid to seek out witches, not all of them were just out to make money. Many believed they really could unmask witches. They had a set of tests which told them if a person was a witch or not. These tests varied, but included listening to the evidence of local people, checking for a 'Devil's Mark' (a mole or blemish of any other sort) and pricking the accused with a pin (witches did not bleed). A witch-hunter's decision could depend on the actions of others, as this story about a Scottish witch-hunter in Newcastle in 1649 shows:

'Lieutenant Colonel Hobson said, "Surely this woman is not a witch?" The Scotsman said that the townspeople said she was, so he had to test her. In front of everyone he threw her clothes up over her head. All the blood contracted to one part of her body, with fright and shame. The Scotsman ran a pin into her thigh, quickly let her clothes fall and asked why she did not bleed. He then set her aside as a child of the Devil. Lieutenant Colonel Hobson, having seen the way her blood settled, had her called forward again, and had the Scotsman test her again. The blood gushed out and so the witchfinder cleared her and said she was not a child of the Devil.'

## Anne Chattox

For many years, the people of Pendle, Lancashire were sure Anne Chattox was a witch. They had tried hard not to displease her. One man, John Device, was so scared that he promised to give her a sack of ground oats each year, as long as she did not harm him, his family or his possessions. One year he missed payment, fell sick and died, convinced that she had cursed him. A few years later Anne was one of several women, and one man, tried as witches in 1612. The man, one of the few men ever to be tried as a witch, was James Device, son of John.

## Work it out!

1  a  What supernatural explanations did people give for mysterious disasters?

   b  Why might they choose one explanation rather than another?

2  Think carefully about the kind of person who was most likely to be accused of witchcraft.

   Draw a picture of this type of person and label the 'suspect' things about him or her.

3  a  Why did people make witchcraft accusations?

   b  How did they decide who to accuse?

4  Read **Guilty consciences?**

   a  Why might the accusers of Margery Stanton have had guilty consciences?

   b  How would seeing her as a witch make them feel less guilty?

37

# Matthew Hopkins, witchfinder!

**M**ost accusations of witchcraft in Britain were made by the supposed victims of witches. In other parts of Europe, witch-hunting was done by professional 'witchfinders'. The few British witchfinders worked mainly in the 1640s and 1650s. The most notorious of these was Matthew Hopkins.

## Who was Matthew Hopkins?

We know very little about Hopkins' childhood. He claims to have been the son of a minister in Suffolk and by 1644 was living in Manningtree, Essex. Some people, who have studied his books and the way he presented evidence at witch trials, think he may have trained as a lawyer.

Hopkins claimed that he decided to become a witchfinder after hearing of a group of witches living near to his home. He certainly believed in God and the Devil, and feared both. He had read, and accepted as true, James I's book on witchcraft, *Demonology*.

Once Hopkins was famous, he was sent for to root out witches in some towns. However, in most cases, he wrote to the magistrates of towns where he thought there might be witches and offered to work for them. Other witchfinders at the time were paid £1 a suspect. Hopkins was never paid less than £5.

## SOURCE A

*Greetings, your Worship,*

*I have today been sent a letter to come to your town to search for evil disposed persons, called witches. I hear your Minister is against us, through ignorance. I will come (God willing) to hear his views, for I have heard others speak against the discovery of witches from the pulpit. They were soon forced to change their minds. I shall visit your town suddenly. I would like first to know how I shall be met, for if there are many set against us, then I shall not come. I shall go instead where people will accept me with thanks and payment.*

*your servant,*

*Matthew Hopkins.*

**A letter written in 1645 by Hopkins to the magistrate of an Essex town.**

To Hopkins and many others, it seemed logical that, if the Devil was real, then he could tempt people and lead them astray. This idea was even used in courts as a reason for people's actions. This picture came with an account of a trial in Scotland, where the accused was said to have made a pact with the Devil – the black creature on the left.

**SOURCE B**

# Hopkins' methods

Hopkins wrote a pamphlet in 1647, which outlined his methods and tried to justify them. Here are some of the questions and answers there:

**Query 8:** Once the Devil's mark has been discovered, why must the suspects be tortured and kept from sleep? Surely this will distract them and make them say anything?

**Answer:** It was thought best to do this, because if they were kept awake they would call their familiars to them, which often happened. The magistrates let us do this. The witches never complained till they were in jail together. When they were put in together they decided to complain to the magistrates. Since then, the magistrates have ordered that they be not kept awake. Perhaps it was their consciences that did not let them sleep.

**Query 9:** Beside keeping them awake, why did you force them to keep walking up and down until their feet were blistered and they confessed?

**Answer:** They were only walked to keep them awake while watching them. If they were allowed to sit or lie down, then their familiars came. This scared the watchers and cheered the witches up. Since it was forbidden to keep them awake, they have been allowed to sleep.

**Query 10:** What about the cruel trial of these poor creatures, by tying them and heaving them into the water. I mean 'swimming'. Is this not both illegal and immoral?

**Answer:** The Devil tells them to agree to this, that they may be cleared. It was never brought as evidence in a trial. King James' *Demonology* gives this as a sure test for a witch. Many ministers (whom I respect) have condemned swimming, so it is no longer done.

Hopkins at work, from his book on witchcraft, first printed in 1647.

# Hopkins' end

In all, Hopkins had about 400 people tried as witches. Over half of these were convicted and hanged. In 1645 various clergymen and others began to question his methods and the size of his fees. Public support for Hopkins began to slow. Magistrates were discouraged from employing him. In the autumn of 1646, Hopkins retired. He wrote a pamphlet to justify his methods, but he never worked again. Within a year he was dead of tuberculosis.

# Work it out!

1 Why do you think Matthew Hopkins became a witchfinder? Explain this.

2 Why do you think Hopkins wrote to the magistrates in towns before he went there?

3 What do his letter and the extract from his book say he felt about the ministers who opposed him?

4 Having read the extract from his book, why do you think Hopkins retired?

# Cony-catchers: a real threat?

In the 1590s, several hugely successful pamphlets were published. They told of a criminal underworld, where every beggar, pedlar and thief belonged to a countrywide organisation with its own language, laws and support system. These pamphlets, written by professional authors like Robert Greene, all claimed to be revealing a 'true' view of the criminal underworld. They called its members 'cony-catchers' – tricksters. The pamphlets fed off each other, each saying, 'the underworld exists, but my colleague has got details wrong, here is the real truth'. So, did Greene and the rest really write from experience? And was there a criminal underworld that every beggar and thief belonged to? Study the following information.

## A JP's story

Thomas Harman was a Justice of the Peace in Kent. One of his jobs was to act as a magistrate in local trials, prosecuting beggars and other vagrants (people wandering around the country without work). He says that his pamphlet was written from his own experience:

'I have talked daily with these wily wanderers, men and women, boys and girls, from whom I have learned about and have come to understand their detestable dealing. With fair flattering words, money and good cheer [food and drink], I have found out much about their wanderings and ways.'

Surely we can believe a JP? Many historians have. Harman gives a very detailed breakdown of the various sorts of beggar. He outlines their special language.

He talks about the huge gangs they moved around in. Was he making it up?

The situation is more complicated than that. Harman had a copy of Awdeley's pamphlet (1561). It was this that started him thinking about the criminal underworld. So, he began his enquiries, already believing that there was an underworld and that every beggar belonged to it. He could well have written his book to help people understand that beggars could be tricksters. This does not mean he wrote the truth.

## A written tradition

Robert Greene's pamphlets were the most successful. They were the ones that sparked off many others. It is possible to trace Greene's sources through time:

- **1591** *A Notable Discovery of Cozenage*, Greene's first, cony-catching pamphlet.
- **1566** *A Caveat For Common Cursitors*, written by Thomas Harman, a Justice of the Peace. This was probably Greene's source of information, reprinted in 1592, after Greene's success.
- **1561** *The Fraternity of Vagabonds*, written by John Awdeley, a printer who published pamphlets.
- **1552** *A Manifest Detection of Diceplay*, written by Gilbert Walker, about whom we know nothing.
- **1535** *The Highway to the Spital House*, written by Robert Copeland, another printer who wrote and published pamphlets.

These books have connections to German books, printed earlier and definitely literature, not real investigative journalism.

SOURCE A

A
Notable Discouery of Coosenage.
Now daily practised by sundry lewd persons, called 'Connie-catchers, and Crosse-byters.

Plainly laying open those pernitious sleights that hath brought many ignorant men to confusion.

Written for the generall benefit of all Gentlemen, Citizens, Aprentifes, Country Farmers and yeomen, that may hap to fall into the company of such coosening companions.

With a delightfull difcourse of the coofnage of Colliers.

Nafcimur pro patria.   By R. Greene, Maifter of Arts.

LONDON
Printed by Thomas Searlet for Thomas Nelson.
1 5 9 2.

# Some of Harman's 'Beggars' Brotherhood'

Harman describes 23 sorts of beggars. Awdeley described 25. Harman uses the same groups as Awdeley and, more often than not, the same names.

## The Ruffler

The Ruffler is the chief beggar. Either he has fought in the wars, or served a great lord. Weary of well-doing, he chooses the idle life. He may show you wounds, supposedly war-wounds, but really from a brawl in an inn. True soldiers are killed in battle, or are too proud to beg from door to door. Rufflers give orders to all the rest, have their pick of all the women and father many children.

## The Prigger of Prancers

Priggers of Prancers steal horses. They wear leather or white wool jackets and carry small sticks. Harman adds: 'I had the best of my horses stolen from my pasture, while the book was first printing.'

## Palliards and their morts

Palliards and their women, called morts, are mostly Welsh and both wear patched cloaks. They beg separately from door to door, carrying fake licences to beg. They put herbs and arsenic on their legs, to raise blisters, full of pus and ill-looking. It dries up soon, and they are well.

## Anglers

Anglers wear wool jackets and ragged trousers which go to points at the knee. They carry a long staff with a small hole in the top. By day they go from house to house begging. At night they attach a hook to the end of their staff and go through the streets, hooking things out of windows. Harman adds: 'I have talked with them, and noticed that they cover the hole in their staff with their hands as they speak. I heard of one angler who hooked the sheets and covers off a sleeping couple, without them noticing.'

## The language

Copeland was the first person to list words from the secret language of beggars. It was Harman who expanded it, and made a special feature of the language:

| | |
|---|---|
| *glaziers* | eyes |
| *duds* | clothes |
| *libbege* | bed |
| *booze* | drink |
| *bene* | good |
| *grannam* | corn |
| *a margery-prater* | a hen |
| *the darkmans* | night |
| *a ken* | a house |

SOURCE B

Nicholas Jennings, a Counterfeit Crank, blistered his legs and ate soap to pretend illness. Harman said he tracked this man down. The engraving shows him as a wealthy man living a rich life and in the beggar's disguise that made him rich.

It is probable that there *was* a criminal class when the cony-catching books were being written. However, it is very difficult to work out its size. This was a time when there were laws about begging and vagrancy (travelling from place to place, without work). While some cony-catching books talked about con-men (who cheated at cards or talked people out of money), others talked of an organisation of beggars and vagrants. So how far does the record of arrests fit the pamphlet view?

In the 1590s the books began to specialise in dishonest beggars or con-men who tricked people in various ways, including cheating at cards. This painting, made some fifty years later, shows that cheating at cards still went on. Look carefully at the man on the left.

## Licensed to beg

The laws on begging and vagrancy changed over time; the punishments varied, as did the groups of people who could be arrested. However, the basic rules stayed the same:

- Beggars were divided into those who were able to work and those who were not.

- Those unable to work were given a licence to beg. The licence operated only in their home town and the countryside around. If they were arrested locally, they had to stay put. If they were arrested in a place that was not their birthplace, they were sent home – their licence was changed to allow them to beg on their way home. Once they got home, they were expected to stay there.

- Those who were fit for work were expected to return to their place of birth and find work or, according to later laws, were given the worst kinds of work. Sometimes, they too were given a licence to allow them to beg on their way home. Once they got home, they were expected to stay there.

SOURCE C

## Views at the time

At the time that these pamphlets were written, most people had similar views on vagrants. They thought that:

- vagrancy was rising rapidly
- vagrants travelled in large, self-supporting groups
- vagrants were also thieves and were often violent
- vagrants were avoiding work, not looking for work.

## A modern view

The historian A.L. Beier studied vagrancy arrests and found that:

- almost 90% of vagrants were travelling in groups of three or less
- about 80% were looking for work, or travelling for family reasons
- about 60% were within 50 miles of home
- about 65% were single men
- about 22% were single women
- about 13% were families
- about 60% were under 21 years old (this shoots up to 90% in London)
- the numbers of people arrested went up in years when the harvests were bad, prices were rising and wages were falling
- the three biggest groups were apprentices and servants, clothworkers, and sailors and soldiers.

## Work it out!

1  Read **A JP's story**. What is there about the way that Harman got his information that makes you think it could be wrong?

   Explain your answer.

2  Read **Some of Harman's 'Beggars' Brotherhood'**.

   a  Which book did Harman read before he did the 'research' for his book?

   b  How are the books similar?

3  Read **Licensed to beg**.

   a  What sorts of people were given licences to beg?

   b  What sorts of people were refused licences to beg?

   c  Why do you think that these laws insisted that everyone, licensed to beg or not, had to go back to the place where they were born and stay there?

4  Read **Views at the time** and **A modern view**.

   Do A.L. Beier's findings support the views of people at the time?

   Explain your answer.

5  A.L. Beier's findings are based on records of arrests. In Elizabethan times arrests were made by local constables, who were poorly paid. They were often older men who could find no other work. How might the fact that Beier is studying only arrests affect his findings on:

   a  the size of vagrant groups?

   b  the kinds of people in these groups?

   c  what they were doing on the road?

   Explain your answer.

6  Why might people at the time have found it comforting to think that beggars were not really people in need of help?

# Discovering a new world or destroying other cultures?

## European expansion 1450–1750

### A whole new world

In 1450, Europeans only really knew about a third of the world, centred around Europe. Most of Africa, Asia and the Americas were unknown. By 1600 they were drawing maps that showed, fairly accurately, over two-thirds of the world.

Rich Europeans bought foreign goods such as pepper, ivory and dyes from India; silk, porcelain, musk and ginger from China; and cinnamon, nutmeg and sapphires from Indonesia. Cities such as Venice and Genoa in Italy grew rich through trade. Marco Polo was an Italian trader and explorer. He was unusual because he had travelled as far as China.

Most traders just bargained with other traders, closer to home, and goods came step-by-step to Europe.

### Fancy goods

Why did rich people want these foreign goods? To be different from most other people is the simple answer. The peasants could afford only woollen cloth; the rich wanted silk. Most people had plain green and brown clothes; the rich wanted bright blues, vivid yellows and rich reds. Anyone seeing these colours would know the owner was rich, very rich. But rich people wanted more than fancy cloth and bright dyes. They wanted spices from the East to make their food taste better. They wanted perfumes to cover their own smell and the smell of those around them, because people bathed infrequently.

Marco Polo claimed to have found China, but people didn't know whether explorers would be able to find it again. The explorer Christopher Columbus tried to reach it, sailing westwards in 1492.

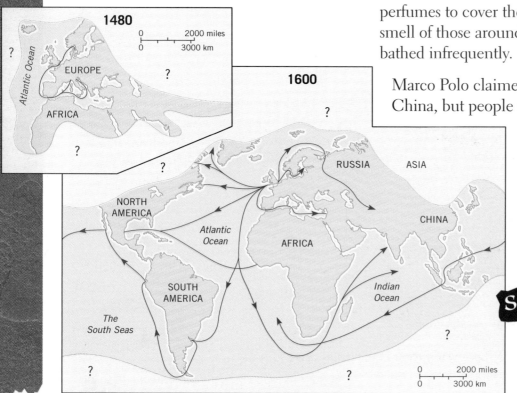

**SOURCE A**

— English trade and exploration routes

? Unknown territory

44  **The known and the unknown world in 1480 and 1600.**

# Why explore?

What were the main factors pushing the explorers? Let us look at the possible motives of one explorer – Christopher Columbus.

Money always has been something that persuades people to do things, even things that are dangerous. Money may have pushed Columbus to set off to look for China in 1492.

A second reason that may have made Columbus want to travel was religion. Columbus wanted to convert people to Christianity. He hoped to use some of the fortune he would make to raise an army to regain Jerusalem from the Muslims.

The desire to be remembered after his death was another reason for Columbus' voyages. Columbus also wanted to be given the title 'Admiral of the Ocean' which was hereditary. This means that he would pass the title on to his children.

## SOURCE B

O most excellent gold! Whoever has gold has a treasure, which gives him the power to get what he wants. It lets him do what he wants in the world and even helps souls into heaven.

**Columbus persuaded the King and Queen of Spain to give him three ships because he promised them wealth.**

# New technology

New inventions and developments in technology made sailors' journeys easier. The compass and the astrolabe (a device which helps measure distance from the Equator) helped sailors find their positions and plan directions, using the sun and the stars. The compass was described as 'the greatest single step ever made in the aid of navigation'.

Some explorers borrowed ideas from the Arabs, like the use of a large, triangle-shaped sail, which made ocean-sailing a possibility. Columbus used this technology with his three ships: the *Pinta*, the *Niña* and the *Santa María*. Men also became more skilled at drawing maps and chart-making. However, it was the fact that Columbus miscalculated the distance from Europe to Asia that made him believe he could complete the journey from Spain to China. It is also ironic that Columbus never knew that he had discovered the new continent of America, insisting to the end that he had reached Asia.

## SOURCE C

Columbus wanted to fill his empty ships with gold before returning home. This engraving shows Indians having their hands and noses cut off for not supplying enough gold.

# Who went where when?

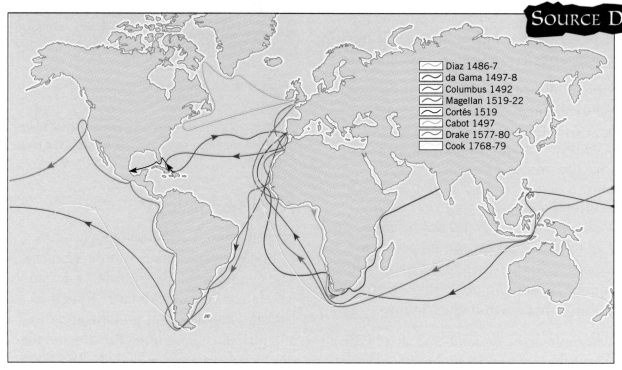

Diaz 1486-7
da Gama 1497-8
Columbus 1492
Magellan 1519-22
Cortés 1519
Cabot 1497
Drake 1577-80
Cook 1768-79

**Journeys made by the great explorers.**

The table below shows some of the most famous explorers and where they went.

| Name | Funded by | Date | Destination |
|------|-----------|------|-------------|
| Bartholomew Diaz | Portuguese | 1486–7 | South Africa |
| Vasco da Gama | Portuguese | 1497–8 | India |
| Christopher Columbus | Spanish | 1492 | West Indies |
| Ferdinand Magellan | Spanish | 1519–22 | Circled the world |
| Hernando Cortés | Spanish | 1519 | Mexico |
| John Cabot | English | 1497 | Newfoundland |
| Francis Drake | English | 1577–80 | Circled the world |
| James Cook | English | 1768–79 | Australia |

# The consequences of discovery

What were the consequences of these voyages? The most obvious effect on the people who were 'discovered' by the explorers was that they lost control over their own lives. This was especially so in the Americas, as the European settlers were not willing to live in close harmony with the native peoples. The natives had riches that the Europeans wanted. The invaders just assumed they had a right to take over land and natural resources. The Spanish found the Aztecs, an ancient Mexican tribe, and their gold. The Spanish believed that the gold now belonged to them.

When Columbus arrived on the island of Hispaniola (now called Haiti), he felt he could demand whatever he wanted – and he wanted gold. He forced every man and woman aged over 14 years to bring him a set amount of gold every 3 months. Those who brought the gold were given a token; those who did not had their hands chopped off. As the island had very little gold, Columbus' demands were impossible to meet. Hundreds of islanders were murdered; the rest committed mass suicide, using a poison from the cassava plant. It is estimated that half the island's population died in this way.

Cortés and his men explored Central America and destroyed the Aztec Empire. They took over the land and divided it up among themselves. They made the native Indians work for them and bring them tributes (tributes are offerings or payments). They also made the Indians become Catholics.

The Spanish also took over the Mayan Empire in the same way. They wanted gold but brought with them smallpox, typhoid and measles. Many Mayans died from these diseases, or through overwork on such schemes as building churches.

The long-term effects of the discovery of the New World were very much the same as the short-term ones. Europeans took over and exploited these new lands. This was really the start of the great European empire-building that reached its height in the nineteenth century.

SOURCE E

A painting showing Cortés and his men. The painter was a Mexican revolutionary and did not agree with what the explorers did to the native people.

## The spoils of discovery

As we have seen, silks, dyes, spices and porcelain had been available for many centuries, but the traders brought many new goods. Indeed, 60% of all types of crops grown in the world today come from the Americas. In Britain, by 1750, you could buy apricots, avocados, bananas, beetroot, kidney beans, melons, peaches, peanuts, pineapples, potatoes, tomatoes, turkeys and gin. The main goods, however, were chocolate, coffee, cotton, sugar, tea and tobacco. It became the height of fashion to drink coffee or hot chocolate in one of the new coffee-houses, whilst smoking a pipe and reading one of the new newspapers. Some rich people also had another fashionable toy – a black slave to wait on them.

# The slave trade

Many of the native inhabitants of the new lands died or were killed. The Europeans replaced them with people from Africa. Hispaniola had lost all of its native population by 1540. The Spanish simply brought over black slaves from Africa – without a thought for their well-being.

In 1563, Queen Elizabeth I stated that it was wrong to enslave another man; a year later she knighted John Hawkins for his profitable enterprise – dealing in slaves. The slave trade was to be one of the darkest chapters in our history. The rise of the English ports of Liverpool and Bristol, and Glasgow in Scotland, was due, in part, to the slave trade.

The slave trade is often called the Triangular Trade. Ships would set sail from Britain carrying poor-quality goods, such as iron bars, cast-off clothing, brandy or cowrie shells. Africans used these shells as money. The Europeans used them as ballast (to keep the boat upright in the sea) so it was a bonus to be able to use them as currency when they arrived at their destination.

John Hawkins' crest. He was proud of his business as a slave trader and designed this new coat of arms. Notice the slave at the top of the crest.

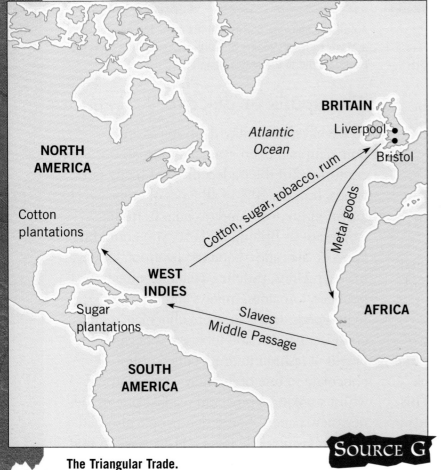

SOURCE G

The Triangular Trade.

The traders bought human beings – slaves. The tribes living on the coast of Africa were encouraged to capture members of other tribes from deep within the jungle to sell to the traders. These slaves were shipped across the Atlantic to be sold to the plantation owners in the West Indies or mainland America. The profit was used to buy cotton, sugar, tobacco or rum to take back home. Before these goods could be put on board the ship they had to be disinfected, and the rats that had been aboard were removed.

Being part of the ship's crew was not a pleasant experience. The sailors on these journeys were usually criminals, escapees from jail, debtors or those on the run from the law. The Middle Passage was the worst part of the journey.

Take the slave ship *Hannibal* as an example. Her Captain bought over 700 black slaves to be taken to Barbados. Before he had even set out, 12 had committed suicide by jumping overboard. The journey took 34 days. A further 334 slaves died on the journey. Only 372 arrived alive in Barbados, where they were sold for an average of £19 a head.

Life below deck would have been very, very hot. The deck might have been covered in blood and mucus. The slaves were chained up and put in the smallest possible space. The ship owners believed that the more slaves they could fit in, the less it mattered if some died on the way.

Why did this trade continue? Profit. People stood to make huge profits. The problem with making lots of money is that people tend to lose sight of what is right and what is wrong. It became all right to deal in human cargo.

## Work it out!

1 Look at maps of the known world in 1480 and 1600.
   a What continents were unknown in 1480?
   b What continents were unknown in 1600?
   c Use the maps to explain why Columbus might have been so sure that South America was, in fact, China.

2 Produce a series of personal profiles of the explorers. You should include the following:
   • Name
   • Age
   • Dates of travel
   • Country where the voyage started
   • Destination
   • A picture
   • One interesting fact about the explorer.

The table on page 46 will help you get started. To complete the task you will need to do some of your own research. Ask your teacher or librarian to help you.

3 Make a table with two columns like the one below. Fill in the table, using the information from this chapter. An example is given.

4 Give at least three reasons why Columbus went on his voyages of discovery. For each reason say why it was an important factor.

5 a Write a list of good things that you think the explorers did for the native people they encountered.
   b Write a list of bad things that you think the explorers did for the native people they encountered.
   c Now decide: did the native people benefit from the arrival of the explorers?

6 a What is the Triangular Trade?
   b How did the Triangular Trade work?
   c Copy the diagram of the Triangular Trade into your book, making sure you label each stage correctly.

7 Ports which were involved in the Slave Trade often have museums of local history. However, very few of these museums devote much space to the Slave Trade, even though it was this trade that was the basis of the cities' wealth. Can you think why this is?

| Item discovered in the New World | Without this, we would not have |
|---|---|
| Potato | Chips |

# 1500–1600: a century of religious controversy

## The Reformation

From 1500 onward, there was growing discontent among Christians with the corruption in the Catholic Church. People protested that they wanted reforms. The Pope refused to reform and people began to form their own Christian groups, separate from the Catholic Church. They called themselves Protestants. This split in Christian worship divided nations, even families.

## Henry VIII, Defender of the Faith

Henry VIII was a very religious man. He was a devout Catholic, so much so that he wrote a book denouncing the attacks on the Pope. The Pope was so impressed and pleased with Henry that he called him Fidei Defensor, Latin for 'Defender of the Faith'. He was glad to have the support of a strong and important nation in Europe.

## The break with Rome

A clash was brewing between Henry and the Pope. Henry had been married to Catherine of Aragon since 1509. They had just one child, a daughter called Mary. Henry wanted a son to rule after him, but Catherine was getting too old to have any more children. Henry asked the Pope to give him a divorce so that he could marry a new wife, Anne Boleyn. Anne was already pregnant and, according to all the experts, carrying a male heir.

Pope Clement VII refused Henry's request. Why? One reason was that the Pope was the prisoner of the Spanish King, Charles I. Charles would not allow his aunt, Catherine of Aragon, to be divorced from Henry and lose all of her privileges and standing in society. Henry had to have a divorce. So, as the Pope would not give him one, he broke away from the Catholic Church and made himself head of the Church in England. The Church promptly gave him a divorce. Not all of Henry's friends and advisers believed that he was doing the right thing. Sir Thomas More, one of Henry's closest advisers, was executed for refusing to support Henry's actions.

## Closing the monasteries

Henry loved to party, hold tournaments and fight wars. To afford this, he needed money, badly. The Church was very rich. As Head of the English Catholic Church, Henry could take some of that wealth for himself.

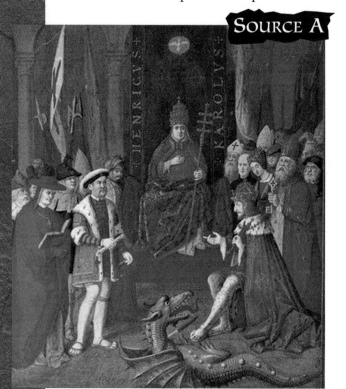

**SOURCE A**

Henry VIII as Defender of the Faith

The monasteries owned about 10% of all the land in England and were also rich. Henry accused the monks and nuns of a wide variety of crimes: from the very minor crime of eating too much, to the much worse sin of having sex. Thomas Cromwell sent out inspectors to each of the monasteries to ask local people questions that would show how bad the monks and nuns were. With his evidence, much of it hearsay (gossip) or simply made up, Henry closed down all of the monasteries. Henry melted down the gold from the altars; he sold the lead from the roofs and the glass from the windows. Then he sold off the land. Henry took charge of the Church to get his divorce. He closed the monasteries to make money.

It was not his intention to change the religious beliefs of the ordinary person. Even though Henry broke from the Catholic Church in Rome, he remained a Catholic. He never became a Protestant. Henry made Parliament pass the Six Articles in 1539. These were based on Catholic ideas. Henry executed Catholics for the crime of treason (actions against the King or government).

He executed Protestants for heresy (not believing in the Catholic Church).

## The rise of Protestantism

Henry VIII's third wife, Jane Seymour, gave him a son: Edward. Henry became more Protestant with age, and Edward was brought up as a Protestant. When Edward became King he introduced even more Protestant reforms. The Latin Bible and Prayer Book were replaced with English versions. Services were held in English. Priests were now allowed to marry. The elaborate wall-paintings in the churches were whitewashed. Altars were replaced by simple tables; statues of Jesus on the cross and of the Virgin Mary were thrown away. The Protestants replaced Mass by Communion. Catholic congregations had believed they were actually eating Jesus' body and drinking his blood, when they took bread and wine during Mass. The Protestant Communion was a service of remembrance and, for them, bread and wine were just symbols.

SOURCE B

bells

lead from the roof

windows

gold and silver goods from the altar

stone from the walls

monastery lands

**The valuable parts of a monastery.**

# A return to Catholicism?

The death of Edward caused the Protestants problems. Edward's half-sister (Catherine of Aragon's daughter) Mary, succeeded him. Mary was a devout Catholic and was bitter about her treatment, and that of her mother, since England's split with Rome. Mary tried to turn back the clock, to return to a time before Henry had split from the Pope. Mary wanted to turn the country back into a Catholic nation but she was wise enough not to try to reclaim the monastic lands. People had to worship in the Catholic way, though. Those who would not change were burned at the stake as heretics (non-Catholics). With 284 burnings in 5 years, Mary averaged over one a week.

Mary had a few factors in her favour. Firstly, Protestantism was still a new religion. Most people were happy to return to the beliefs they had always had. Secondly, the English people supported Mary and wanted her as their Queen. After Edward died, his Protestant advisers tried to put Lady Jane Grey on the throne instead of Mary. Within 9 days Jane had lost her throne and many Protestant leaders fled abroad.

There were also a few factors against Mary. Firstly, there were still many Protestants in England, a source of possible rebellion. Secondly, Mary could not reclaim the land lost by the monasteries. Too many important people, whose support she needed, now owned this land. Thirdly, Mary had married Philip II of Spain, and many people were very unhappy about being ruled by a foreigner. Finally, Mary had no children. She would be replaced by her half-sister Elizabeth who was a Protestant.

## A religious 'middle way'

By the time Mary I died, she was very unpopular. In fact, most people were relieved when she died and Elizabeth replaced her. Mary had turned people against Catholicism by her extreme behaviour. When Elizabeth became Queen in 1558 she tried to create a Church that was a 'middle way'. Under Elizabeth, the Prayer Book in English was brought back, priests were allowed to marry and people were encouraged to read the Bible. But Elizabeth was not the 'Head' of the Church; she made herself 'Governor'. This, she hoped, would please the Catholics. Elizabeth's Church was neither

SOURCE C

Execution of Thomas Cranmer. As Archbishop of Canterbury, Cranmer had helped Henry split from Rome and then, with Edward, rushed through changes to Protestantism. Mary had him put to death.

Catholic nor extreme Protestant. Historians are not sure what religious beliefs Elizabeth herself held. However, her 'middle way' was successful, though she was always aware of the dangers presented to her by the Catholics.

When Elizabeth came to the throne, the Pope stated that she, daughter of Henry and Anne Boleyn, was not the legitimate ruler of England. The Pope said Elizabeth's cousin, Mary Queen of Scots, was the rightful heir. Despite the fact Mary was a queen, Elizabeth eventually had her executed – Elizabeth believed that Mary had been involved in a plot against her.

Mary's execution was one of the factors that led to the attempted invasion by the Spanish Armada. Philip II of Spain saw it as his duty to return England to the Catholic Church. His plan was well worked out and included raising an army of 45,000 English Catholics. But the plan failed.

## Effects of a century of change

The effect on the ordinary citizen of all these religious changes and upheavals was to undermine the established Church.

Religious groups became splintered. Never again would the nation be united by religion. Many people believed in the new anti-establishment churches, such as the Puritans. The ordinary people still believed in God, just not the same God as their betters.

## Work it out!

1  a  Give as many examples as you can showing that Henry VIII was a good Catholic.

   b  Give as many examples as you can showing that Henry VIII was a bad Catholic.

   c  Now decide if Henry VIII was a good or bad Catholic.

2  Explain how the monasteries provided a source of income for Henry VIII.

3  Mary I's reign is sometimes called 'Turn or Burn'. Why do you think it was given this name?

4  Create a timeline that shows the main events mentioned here and which happened between 1500 and 1600. Use your timeline to help you explain why conflict with the Catholic Church was so important between these dates.

# The poor in Elizabethan times

## How hard was life?

Throughout history, there have always been rich people and poor people. But in Elizabethan times the number of very poor people was rising, while some institutions that had looked after them had been closed down.

The reasons for the rising number of poor in Elizabethan times are many and complex. People at the time blamed poverty and unemployment on such things as the enclosure of land; gambling by the poor; overspending by the rich; the wars with Spain; general greed; and rising prices.

## Rising population, rising prices

However, historians now believe the main reason was a growing population. The population of England was 2.5 million in 1520. It was to rise to over 5 million by 1680.

The growth in population led to inflation. Inflation is when the prices of goods rise.

In the late 1550s the price of cheaper foodstuffs, more likely to be eaten by the poor, rose more quickly than the price of more expensive foods. The price of manufactured goods rose more slowly still. In effect, this made the poor poorer, but the rich better off and able to afford more luxury goods. An ox cost £1 6s 8d (£1.33) in 1500; the same ox cost £3 11s 6d (£3.58) in 1600. The wages of craftsmen were set at 6d a day in 1514, by 1600 this had risen to 12d a day.

Life for a labourer and his family was a constant struggle. Labourers were either tied to one employer, who provided them with work and their home, or were forced to wander the country looking for work at times when extra workers were needed – such as harvest time. A labourer could earn 1s (5p) a week in the seventeenth century but it was hard to find regular work. The peak periods were June for weeding; late August for harvest time; and September for hay-making. A labourer might also expect his wife and children to work at these peak periods.

SOURCE A

A woodcut showing the inside of a farm worker's cottage.

They were all in competition with the many unemployed people who travelled the country to find work.

**A picture of poor, blind people. People who could not help their situation, such as people who could not work through disability, were considered to be 'deserving' poor.**

## What caused unemployment?

People at the time blamed the increase in unemployment on the move from labour-intensive crop-growing to sheep farming, which needed far fewer workers. However, historians now agree that inflation in the late 1500s was a more important cause. Unemployment had a major impact on the poor after Henry VIII's closure of the monasteries. Monks and nuns had previously provided help for the poor; now they could not.

## Blame the poor

A survey in 1569 showed that there were 13,000 beggars. The public in Elizabethan times were not very sympathetic to the unemployed. People genuinely believed that beggars did not work because they did not want to. People believed that these vagabonds would rather risk being hanged than find work! Travelling people caused distrust and fear amongst the rest of the population. Initially, severe laws were enforced.

### SOURCE C

*It's the poor who cannot help themselves that I feel sorry for, the aged, the sick, those who cannot find work. But I've no sympathy for sturdy beggars.*

**Sir Thomas Cecil speaking.**

In reality, it was a bigger population chasing fewer jobs that led to genuine unemployment and people moving around looking for work and begging. People were travelling and looking for all kinds of work. The Forest of Dean's iron industry attracted many migrants, as did the flourishing mining industry on the banks of the Tyne.

# Punish the poor

Various laws were passed to make begging unattractive. One such law stated that the first time a person was caught begging, he or she would be whipped; a second offence would lead to an ear being branded; being caught a third time would mean hanging. It was rare for a beggar to remain in an area long enough to suffer hanging! The local population were keen to drive them out of the area, not wanting to know who they were or why they were in trouble.

People were not interested in beggars and their problems. In one Essex parish, the burial register records a 'poor woman which died in a barne at the parsonage whose name we could not learne'.

## Pity the poor

This distrust of the very poor soon gave way to pity. People began to appreciate that the majority of poor people did not want to beg. Local towns could issue licences and badges to make people into 'official' beggars. In 1591, Newcastle upon Tyne issued 137 such badges; this was twice the number of any other town in England. Rich benefactors also left money to the poor in their wills. Not wishing to leave their money to the Church, this was a way of doing 'good' – giving to the English Church was a way of giving to the Tudors, not to charity. In previous times people left money to monasteries, but these were now gone. Almshouses (free or cheap housing financed

SOURCE D

Feeding the poor who were seen as genuinely in need of help.

through charity) were set up for groups such as widows, orphans, the elderly, or wounded servicemen. In 1601 a Poor Law was introduced that made each parish look after its own poor. They did not always do so.

## What next for the poor?

Elizabethan provision for the poor was not widely enforced. The laws were not changed by later rulers; nor were they any more strictly enforced. In 1665, there were reports of the poor having to eat 'baked beasts' blood instead of bread' and 'cats and dogs'. It was also reported that many people 'have been starved to death in holes'.

As the poor were getting poorer, the rich were getting richer. A few thoughtful landowners may have felt the need to look after their tenants: giving them long leases; guaranteeing tenants the right to renew their lease; and providing help in times of emergency. Overall though, landowners stood to gain from the inflation in prices. Firstly, land maintains its value very well. Secondly, the rise in population meant that, with a shortage of housing, people could be forced to pay higher rents. Thirdly, land that had previously been considered unsuitable was now farmed, making landowners even more money.

## Leaving for good

This was a time when many people considered emigrating (leaving the country). By 1700, some 200,000 people had left for America. Many of those who could not escape to the New World tried to eke out an existence in the forests, clearing a patch of land. This was dangerous as they had no right to stay there and could be removed easily. In addition, these forest farmers could be just as affected by bad harvests in their forests as they would have been in their old villages.

The poor rarely were fortunate; they spent most of their time on the poverty line. For some, however, there was an opportunity to better themselves. It was not impossible for a trader to rise to the rank of landowner through hard work; nor was it impossible for a landowner, unable to take advantage of the new opportunities, to lose his land and become one of the landless poor.

## Work it out!

1  a  How much did an ox cost in 1500?

   b  How much did an ox cost in 1600?

   c  Roughly what percentage increase was this?

   d  How much did a craftsman earn in 1514?

   e  How much did a craftsman earn in 1600?

   f  Roughly what percentage increase was this?

   g  Do your answers to parts c and f help to explain one of the causes of poverty in Elizabethan times?

2  a  Who were the 'deserving' poor and who were the vagabonds?

   b  How were these two groups treated differently?

3  a  Make a list of the reasons why the poor became poorer in the reign of Elizabeth.

   b  Give the reasons in order of importance.

   c  Explain why you chose your 'top three'.

# The struggle for power in the seventeenth century

## Who should rule: King or Parliament?

In 1649, at the end of the English Civil War, King Charles I was beheaded in public. Earlier, he had been tried by a Court of Law and he had been found guilty of treason. Charles was not the first King to be executed, but he was the first to be executed legally by his own subjects. Why did this extreme event happen?

## The Cavaliers and the Roundheads

The history book *1066 and All That* says that the English Civil War was 'the utterly memorable struggle between the Cavaliers (wrong but wromantic) and the Roundheads (right but repulsive).' The Cavaliers fought for King Charles and the Roundheads fought for Parliament under Oliver Cromwell.

It is true that people usually see the swashbuckling Cavaliers as romantic and the Roundheads as boring. However, many modern historians agree that England needed to have the Civil War; that the King deserved to be beheaded; that the Cavaliers were wrong and the Roundheads were right. Why is this?

## Monarch and Parliament

Since the Middle Ages, England has had a Parliament. Two groups, the Lords and the Commons, would meet with the monarch (King or Queen) to discuss how to run the country. The Commons had the very important role of raising taxes. Any major expenditure that the King or Queen had, such as going to war, was financed by taxes. Slowly, with few people noticing, Parliament became more powerful, though never as powerful as the monarch.

## The Tudors and Parliament

When the Tudors came to power, they worked *with* Parliament. They gave Parliament greater powers in the expectation that the government would support them in any major policy decision. So, in 1534 Henry VIII was able to get the Act of Supremacy passed by the government and he was named Head of the English Catholic Church.

Elizabeth I believed that Parliament had a right to free speech, even though she did not always agree with what MPs said. She generally had good relations with her parliament, though this was often the result of skilful management by her advisers. There were disagreements, however, such as when she refused to accept a law that banned hunting, cock-fighting and bear-baiting on Sundays. She felt her subjects should be able to enjoy themselves on their day off!

## The Stuarts and Parliament

The most serious disagreement between the Crown and Parliament began when the Stuarts took the English throne in 1603. James I stated that 'it is treason to dispute what a King might do!' James genuinely believed that God had chosen him to be King. He called it his 'Divine Right'.

Henry VIII visiting Parliament.

However, James had to accept Parliament because he needed to raise money through taxes – something only Parliament had the legal right to do. James had been King of Scotland, a very poor country. He loved being able to spend great sums of money. Parliament was not impressed with James and disapproved of his friendship with George Villiers, the newly created Duke of Buckingham.

## Charles I and the long-term causes of the Civil War

When James' son, Charles, succeeded him in 1625, Buckingham continued to have great influence. Parliament began to criticise Charles' advisers, especially Buckingham, and his policies. This caused bad feeling. Parliament also used the tactic of not voting the taxes Charles needed until they had aired their 'grievances'. A lot of bad feeling followed and Charles dissolved Parliament and tried to rule without it.

In the following 11 years, Charles tried to use a variety of money-raising methods, such as granting monopolies to traders and imposing a tax called Ship Money on the entire country. This tax was one of the few that the King could impose legally, but only in coastal areas and only to finance ship-building when preparing for war. Charles used the money for himself, not for the purpose that was intended. Parliament was not happy about losing its tax-raising powers. Equally important, many rich landowners and merchants were not pleased about being taxed heavily.

At the same time as upsetting Parliament, Charles began to alarm the people of England by his moves to restore the Catholic faith. He married a French Catholic and encouraged the Archbishop of Canterbury, William Laud, to introduce practices that were considered Catholic. Charles then made a big mistake. He tried to introduce these changes to the Scottish Church which was far more radically Protestant than the English one. Priests trying to read from Laud's new prayer book were met with riots. Many Scots signed the Covenant (a document in which they promised to keep their Protestant beliefs).

Charles raised an army to invade Scotland, but he was soon in difficulty. Needing some money, he recalled Parliament. John Pym, the leader of the Commons, refused to give Charles any money. Charles dissolved Parliament, but then had to recall it – the Scots had captured Newcastle upon Tyne and were demanding a ransom to give it back.

## Short-term causes – how the war actually started

This, then, was the problem: Charles did not want to rule with Parliament, but he had no choice; he needed the money only Parliament could provide. Parliament knew this and tried to use the money as a lever to force Charles to reform. Neither side would give in to the other, so a war was inevitable.

Pym arrested Charles' two main advisers: Laud and the Earl of Stafford. Charles was powerless to save them, and both were put on trial. Laud was executed. The evidence against Stafford was too weak to convict him. So, Pym decided to pass a Bill of Attainder. This basically said that Stafford was guilty whatever the evidence. Charles reacted in an equally unacceptable manner. Without invitation, he entered the Houses of Parliament to arrest Pym and four of his fellow MPs. They had left earlier, warned by spies of Charles' plans. Charles had gone too far, showing he cared little for the laws and liberties of the people. In August 1642, Charles was driven out of London and raised his standard in Nottingham, a safe royalist town. This meant war. Only one side could win. After a series of battles which the Roundheads won, Charles was arrested and eventually executed.

SOURCE B

Charles I demanding that the five MPs be arrested.

| ROUNDHEADS | Side | CAVALIERS |
|---|---|---|
| Oliver Cromwell | **Leader** | The King, Charles I |
| The House of Commons | **Followers in Parliament** | Most of the House of Lords |
| Puritans (Protestants) | **Religious followers** | High Churchmen and Catholics |
| Industrialists in cities, naval leaders and people from the ports | **Other types of followers** | Old gentry in country areas |
| South and East | **Area of the country where most followers were** | North and West |
| London | **Headquarters** | Oxford |

**The two sides of the English Civil War.**

## What next?

Who would run the country now? The country could not be run by the King alone, nor by Parliament alone. Oliver Cromwell became Lord Protector; he was King in all but name.

This should have been a brilliant victory for Parliament – England was a republic and no longer under the dictatorship (total control) of a tyrannical (harsh and brutal) monarch. At first, Cromwell did try to get Parliament to run the country; the problem was that they did not agree with him about how the country should be ruled. Like Charles had done before him, Cromwell sent home the Parliaments that he did not agree with.

Cromwell tried to rule with a few of his supporters. This was called the 'Rump' Parliament. Even this did not work, so Cromwell divided the country into 11 regions, each ruled by a major-general. The population hated these men. It was not long before people forgot the problems under Charles I and began thinking about the problems under Cromwell instead.

In 1658 Oliver Cromwell died, to be succeeded by his son Richard. People did not like Richard and they wanted the rightful King to come back.

SOURCE C

**This painting shows the execution of Charles I.**

A painting showing the Coronation Procession of Charles II.

## A new king

Charles II, Charles I's son, returned to England in 1660. He was careful in his dealings with Parliament, though he did fall out with the government when MPs passed a law banning all Catholics from public office. However, it was his brother, James, who caused the greatest problem when he took the throne after Charles' death.

It was feared that James II would turn England back to Catholicism. However, in 1688, he was removed from the throne. This time the revolution was bloodless. His daughter, the very Protestant Mary II, and her Protestant husband, William of Orange, replaced James.

## A new way

William and Mary had to sign the Bill of Rights. Basically, this said that the monarch could not interfere with laws passed by Parliament. It also said that the monarch could not raise taxes without Parliament's permission. By 1714, when George I became King of England, Parliament's power was still growing. A group of MPs, called the Cabinet, helped George to rule – he could speak very little English as he had been born and brought up in Germany. Soon, one of the ministers became the head of the Cabinet; he became the 'Prime'

Minister. His name was Sir Robert Walpole. Government as we recognise it today had really begun. In less than 150 years, the roles of the monarch and Parliament had been reversed; however, England seemed to need both to maintain stability.

## Work it out!

1 What is meant by 'the Divine Right of Kings'?

2 Using evidence from this section, say why it was a big mistake for Charles I to try to arrest John Pym and the other four MPs.

3 Design two posters. One should argue that executing Charles I was the right thing to do. The other should argue that his execution was wrong. Put in as many points for each side as you can.

4 Henry VIII (1509–1547) made the laws of the land and expected Parliament to agree to them, without argument.

George I (1714–1727) was expected to accept the laws passed by Parliament without argument.

Choose five important events that happened between these two rulers' lives which explain, in your opinion, why there was a change in the way power was shared between the King and Parliament.

# Glossary

**apprentice** a person who is learning a trade by living and working for several years with someone who is already qualified in that trade.

**bored** pierced.

**catholic** originally meaning 'all-encompassing'. This meant it was the religion of all the people of Western Europe.

**civil war** when the people of one country are divided amongst themselves to the point that they will go to war with each other.

**compass** a magnetic device that is designed to always point north, an invaluable aid for sea travel.

**cowrie shells** found on the beaches of the West Indian isles. They were put on the slave ships as ballast (to keep the ships afloat) and then later sold to the Africans who treasured them highly.

**craftsman** a person who is skilled in making a particular thing, such as shoes or gold cups.

**defeat** to win a victory over your opponent.

**divine right** both King James I and King Charles I believed that they had been chosen by God to be king and so were only answerable to Him and not to Parliament.

**emigration** when people leave their own country to go and live permanently in another country.

**enclosure** originally most fields in England were not fenced by hedges. Enclosure is the process of building fences around the fields so that the individual farmer decides what to grow or keep in them, not just what the whole village wants.

**freeman** freemen rented their land from the lord of the manor. They did not have to work on the lord's land and could move around as they pleased.

**guarderobe** a medieval toilet.

**heresy** this is when you do not accept the religious teachings of the leaders of the Church.

**hero** a brave man, someone who is central to the story of events.

**inflation** when the prices of goods go up.

**legally** within the law.

**Lord of the Manor** the person who controls all the land in a village or group of villages. He is given the land by the king.

**mason** a person who builds things from stone.

**massacre** the killing or injuring of a large number of people or animals.

**merchant** a trader who buys and sells goods (such as silk or spices), sometimes with traders from abroad.

**miracle** something which cannot be easily explained as having happened naturally; from the sudden cure for a sick person to people seeing God or the saints.

**monastery** the place where monks lived. Here they would pray, meditate, teach and look after the needy.

**monopoly** if you are the only person or company that can sell a product or service.

008765

**mystery play** plays performed by groups of craftsmen in towns at religious festivals (for example Easter and Christmas). These plays were performed on the streets and told Bible stories.

**noblemen** men born to a very wealthy family.

**oath** a promise made on something that is holy.

**pilgrimage** a journey to a place which has special religious importance.

**Pope** the head of the Roman Catholic Church, a very powerful and influential man.

**Protestants** people who 'protested' against the teachings and actions of the Catholic Church.

**puritans** these were Protestants who wanted the Church to be very 'pure'. They believed the Church should follow exactly what the Bible said.

**rebellion** an act of rising up against the people who hold power.

**reformation** this is the time/process of 'reforming' or changing the Catholic Church.

**relics** these were items of clothing, ornaments or even parts of a person's body, believed to belong to very religious people. Pilgrims travelled miles to pray to them.

**saint** a person that the Church has said did something especially holy. This could be someone who lived a very good life, but was most often someone killed for their religious beliefs.

**shrine** a place that is special to a saint (such as the place they died) or where something that belonged to a saint is kept.

**silk** a very expensive thread made by worms, originally from China.

**smallpox** a terrible disease that killed millions of Native Americans after the arrival of the Europeans.

**spice** usually the dried seeds of plants that are used to flavour food.

**stationed** where an army or individual is placed.

**treason** when a person tries to plot against the king or queen. Usually it is with the intention of helping another person become the monarch.

**Triangular Trade** the name given to the slave trade, mostly because it used three distinct trading stages: Europe to Africa; Africa to America; and America to Europe.

**uprising** the same as rebellion.

**vagabond** a wanderer, someone without a permanent home.

**vagrant** a tramp.

**villain** a wrong-doer, someone who breaks the law.

**villein** a person who is given his house and land by the lord of the manor in return for work. He cannot leave the manor without permission from the lord.

THOMAS LIBRARY